WILLIAM MORRIS

HIS LIFE AND WORK

WILLIAM MORRIS

HIS LIFE AND WORK

STEPHEN COOTE

GARAMOND

For my mother

First published in the UK by Garamond Publishers Ltd
Strode House, 44–50 Osnaburgh Street, London NW1 3ND

British Library Cataloguing in Publication Data
Coote, Stephen
    William Morris: his life and work.
    1. English visual arts. Morris, William, 1834–1896
    I. Title
    709.2

    ISBN 1–85583–085–X

Picture research by Stephen Coote, assisted by Rachel Cook
Designed by Hilary Norman
Typeset by Tradespools Ltd, Frome, Somerset
Origination by Columbia Offset
Printed and bound in Italy

Frontispiece and title page: *Tulip* fabric by William Morris

CONTENTS

VICTORIAN VALUES

The England in which William Morris grew up was the England of the Great Exhibition: prosperous and confident, yet ostentatious in its new wealth and all too often heedless of the human cost on which success was built. Against such values, and through a life of extraordinary achievement, Morris was to bring to bear his strengths as a designer, a socialist and a visionary. To measure the man we must survey his world, and the Great Exhibition of 1851 provides an excellent vantage point for doing so.

By the middle of the nineteenth century, when Morris was in his teens, an ethic of work, enterprise and ingenuity had made Britain the most powerful nation on earth. The country was the workshop of the world. The social and economic problems of the early 1840s seemed a thing of the past and before the people stretched the prospect of unlimited progress powered by the steam engine and a belief in free trade.

The Prince Consort himself had emphasised these ideals in a speech given to the merchants and bankers of the City of London in which he attempted to raise support for the Great Exhibition. His speech glowed with his confidence. As Albert looked about him at the men who were financing a revolution in world trade, so he thought he could see history fulfilling her destined aim – the realisation of the unity of mankind.

Opposite: The Great Exhibition of 1851 and the Crystal Palace which housed it epitomise those Victorian values of commercialism and design that Morris struggled against throughout his life. Heywood, Higgenbottom and Smith's Crystal Palace wallpaper gives these values garish expression.

Nobody who has paid any attention to the peculiar features of the present era, will doubt for a moment that we are living at a period of most wonderful transition, which tends rapidly to accomplish that great end, to which, indeed, all history points—the realization of the unity of mankind . . . The distances which separate the different nations and parts of the globe are rapidly vanishing before the achievements of modern invention, and we can traverse them with incredible ease . . . Thought is communicated with the rapidity and even the power of lightning. On the other hand, the great principle of division of labour, which may be called the moving power of civilization, is being

Prince Albert's speech to the merchants and bankers of the City of London in which he solicited support for the Great Exhibition is a classic exposition of Victorian optimism and pride in achievement.

extended to all branches of science, industry, and art. Whilst formerly the greatest mental energies strove at universal knowledge, and that knowledge was confined to the few, now they are directed on specialities . . . but the knowledge acquired becomes at once the property of the community at large. The products of all quarters of the globe are placed at our disposal, and we have only to choose which is the best and the cheapest for our purposes, and the powers of production are intrusted to the stimulus of competition and capital. So man is approaching a more complete fulfilment of that great and sacred mission he has to perform in this world . . . I confidently hope that the first impression which the view of this vast collection will produce upon the spectator will be that of deep thankfulness to the Almighty for the blessings He has bestowed upon us already here below.

There was certainly much of which the Prince and the bankers could be proud. A network of railways sped goods across the land. English ships ploughed the seas with their cargoes of trade. The new electric telegraph would soon send messages from continent to continent with something approaching the speed of thought. Commerce, it appeared, was indeed binding the world together in prosperity, progress and peace.

Underlying such hopes lay the forces created by the Industrial Revolution. Mass production based on the division of labour was becoming the order of the day. Manufacture was no longer necessarily prized as a matter of individual craftsmen responsible for each stage in an object's production. To many forward-looking minds, the small workshop had given place to the factory floor, the man of many talents to the industrial labourer knowing perhaps only one skill but producing in combination with his fellows a far greater volume of goods than had ever been dreamed of before. For Prince Albert, the benevolent results of such a change could be seen all around in an ever wider choice of cheap manu-factured goods, in competition and the accumulation of capital. Such progress, he believed, witnessed to the abundance and mercy of God.

While an appeal to the divine was attractive to Victorian piety, the building of the Crystal Palace which housed the Exhibition revealed Victorian enterprise at its most magnificently compe-tent. Nearly two thousand men working with blocks, pulleys and ropes erected three iron columns and two girders every sixteen minutes. Machines on site cut the thirty miles of guttering required, while seventy-six trolleys ran around the grooves these made as the glaziers slid the huge glass panels (the largest yet made) into their correct places. Sixty-three thousand square feet of glass were fitted in a week. This was indeed a triumph of mechanisation, of the use of standard, mass-produced units, and of England's ability to organise vast feats of technology. Eventually, over 100,000 exhibits from across the globe were displayed in nearly a million square feet of capacity.

The immense diversity of the exhibits captured the popular imagination, and an average of nearly 43,000 people a day thronged the Crystal Palace eager to see the fruits of modern industry. The greater part of them was hugely delighted by what they saw. Queen Victoria, confiding to the privacy of her diary, expressed the popular mood when she wrote, '*Such* efforts have been made, and our people have shown *such* taste in their manufactures.'

In an age of manufactures and the machine, it was perhaps the Machinery Court itself that best revealed the source of this royal optimism, even while it showed some of the less desirable foundations on which it rested.

In a great roar of steam, shuttles whirled, pistons heaved, cogs span. Agricultural and printing machines showed the power of mechanisation over muscle. Bright and bulging engines – some of them with the combined power of over seven hundred horses and bizarrely fashioned into Greek, Gothic and even Egyptian styles – roared out their anthem of progress, energy and trade.

In one corner, two small sewing machines, worked by a single girl, ran up six hundred stitches in a minute. In another corner, De la Rue's envelope maker (a particular favourite of the Queen's) produced its wares at the rate of one a second. For the correspondent of the *Illustrated London News*, the envelope machine '. . . closely followed several actual movements of the human form divine'.

The magazine's illustration tells a grimmer story. The attendants working the machine are two children. One is so small that he has to stand on a plinth in order to reach his work. The engraving is a stark reminder that it was only four years since an Act of Parliament had reduced child labour in the textile factories to ten hours a day, and less than a decade since Lord Shaftsbury's campaigns had abolished the employment of juveniles in the mines. A careful study of the objects in the Great Exhibition thus reveals the complex web of social, economic and even political relationships in which the Victorians were enmeshed, and so illustrates that design and manufacture can never be wholly separated from the society that produces them.

Below: *De La Rue's envelope maker was much admired, but this engraving from* The Illustrated London News *points to the child labour and exploitation that underlay much Victorian commercial success.*

A nine-year-old child of a factory operative that has grown up in want, privation, and changing conditions, in cold and damp, with insufficient clothing and unwholesome dwellings, is far from

In The Condition of the Working Classes in England *Engels painted a terrible picture of misery.*

having the working strength of a child brought up under healthier conditions. At nine years of age it is sent into the mill to work $6^1/_2$ hours (formerly 8, earlier still, 12 to 14, even 16 hours) daily, until the thirteenth year; then twelve hours until the eighteenth year. The old enfeebling influences continue, while the work is added to them. It is not to be denied that a child of nine years, even an operative's child, can hold out through $6^1/_2$ hours' daily work, without any one being able to trace visible bad results in its development directly to this cause; but in no case can its presence in the damp, heavy air of the factory, often at once warm and wet, contribute to good health; and, in any case, it is unpardonable to sacrifice to the greed of an unfeeling bourgeoisie the time of children which should be devoted solely to their physical and mental development, and to withdraw them from school and the fresh air in order to wear them out for the benefit of the manufacturers.

We have seen that one of the key factors in the society of 1851 was a belief in the progress fostered by industrialisation. That progress was tangible, new, powerful and frighteningly raw. If it demanded to be celebrated, it was also required to disguise itself. It did so in a number of ways.

One of the chief of these was to associate a modern item with a Utopian fantasy, a Never-never Land. Here one of the quintessential objects of 1851 comes into its own: *The Daydreamer* easy chair of papier-mâché designed by H. Fitz Cook for Jennens and Betteridge. The description from the Exhibition catalogue provides a first approach to this fascinatingly monstrous item:

> The chair is decorated at the top with two winged thoughts – the one with bird-like pinions, and crowned with roses, representing happy and joyous dreams, the other with leather bat-like wings – unpleasant and troubled ones. Behind is displayed Hope, under the figure of the rising sun. The twisted supports of the back are ornamented with poppy, heartsease, convolvulus and snowdrop, all emblematic of the subject. In front of the seat is a shell . . . and on either side of it, pleasant and troubled dreams are represented by figures. At the side is seen a figure of Puck, lying asleep in a labyrinth of foliage . . . The style of the ornament is Italian.

Below: *The 'Day Dreamer Easy Chair' symbolises the pursuit of opulent vulgarity so characteristic of the objects displayed in the Great Exhibition.*

What this description immediately makes clear is the importance attached to swathing *The Daydreamer* chair in allegorical significance. Fantasy must be given a pedigree. In an age when every picture told a story, so, it seemed, must every piece of furniture.

The floral ornaments on the twisted supports suggest a second important feature of the designs of 1851: the pursuit of naturalistic detail. An audience relatively unsophisticated in aesthetic matters but having a high regard for scientific accuracy took pleasure in what could easily be evaluated and admired for its accuracy and technological finish. In numerous pieces from the Great Exhibition – from dessert dishes delicately if improbably balanced on the stems of electroplated lily leaves to carpets and fabrics hideously attempting to suggest the riotous abundance of nature – this pursuit of illusion was much admired. Ornament had become conspicuous artifice, a flamboyant display rather than a delightful but disciplined adjunct.

Not all the visitors to the Great Exhibition however were pleased by such items and the world they suggested. Among the six million who came to see the displays was a widow from the genteel village of Walthamstow on the outskirts of London. With her Mrs Morris brought her oldest son William, born on 24 March 1834, and a young man destined to become one of the central figures in the Victorian opposition to the Crystal Palace and what it stood for.

Mrs Morris had been left in comfortable circumstances. During a successful career in the City, her husband had had the good fortune to buy shares in a Devon copper mine. The mine proved rich beyond the speculators' dreams, and Mr Morris's initial investment of a little under £300 soon rose to close on £200,000. Prosperity gave way to wealth, and the family, which in 1840 had moved from the comfort of Elm House, Walthamstow, to the Georgian magnificence of nearby Woodford Hall, now enjoyed what luxuries they chose.

Three years after the move, Mr Morris, always a keen medievalist, felt the need for a coat of arms and a motto suitable to his position. Beneath three lucky horseshoes appeared the Latin inscription 'Peace and Liberty'. As Morris himself was later to be all too keenly aware, these were hopes reared on a prosperity in which the exploited Devon miners themselves had no share. He was from the start enmeshed in the cruel disparities of Victorian England.

In his earliest years, Morris was a delicate child, and although his constitution was later to be of the most robust and able to endure hours of strenuous and exacting work, there were many days of infant illness sustained by calves-foot jelly and beef tea. It was, perhaps, such days that nurtured his early fondness for books, and by the age of seven he was enjoying the medieval panoply and high adventure in the novels of Walter Scott. The seeds of the romantic man of letters were being sown.

Meanwhile, healthy exercise during periods of recuperation fostered other interests. Woodford Hall was surrounded by a 50 acre park and a farm of twice that size which stretched down the Roding valley to the edge of Epping Forest. By riding, shooting, fishing and walking here, Morris came to know the details of the landscape intimately. Even as an old man he could recall the magic of pollarded hornbeams fronting the woodlands, and in *News from Nowhere*, his literary masterpiece, he was again to evoke, '. . . the wide green sea of the Essex marshland, with the great domed line of the sky, and the sun shining down in one flood of peaceful light over the long distance'. Such a deep, sensuous response to nature was to be one of the mainstays of Morris's life – a constant theme, a constant source of renewal.

In the garden of Woodford Hall itself Morris had his own plot to cultivate, and the boy spent hours among the delicate lacings of plants and flowers and the bright perching birds. All of these would later reappear on his wallpapers and fabrics with the variety of an insistent, potent motif. Indeed, a sense of the hushed magic of old and tapestried buildings was already wakened in him by visits to Queen Elizabeth's Hunting Lodge at Chingford Hatch where 'a room hung with faded greenery' inspired many of his later designs.

Then there were the churches. The young Morris rode out eagerly to explore the details of their medieval architecture and enjoy the crisp yet flowing details of gesture and fabric in the monumental brasses erected by earlier generations of knights and merchants. When, at the age of eight, his father took him to Canterbury Cathedral, Morris thought the gates of heaven had opened to him.

Nature and history were both fundamental to Morris and were closely intertwined. Such pleasures, discovered with elated boyish delight, were to help form the vast resources of his pictorial imagination and, as his thought matured, so they gave him a sense of other values: a feeling for craftsmanship and of joy in making that were to shape his criticism of Victorian society.

Now however, after the death of his father in 1847, Morris had to be prepared to enter that world. It was decided he should attend Marlborough College, 'a new and very rough school' as it turned out, where the relative lack of formal education allowed him to pursue his own concerns. Morris himself was later to declare that he 'learnt next to nothing' at Marlborough 'for indeed next to nothing was taught'.

It was, perhaps, the best schooling he could have had. While Morris eventually acquired sufficient Latin and Greek to be able as a man to translate the works of Virgil and Homer, the hours of unregulated freedom left him at liberty to wander the soft and ancient chalklands, to indulge the aristocratic and High Church tastes encouraged by the school chapel, and to study the books on archaeology and Gothic architecture in the library.

Morris had an exceptional ability to absorb such knowledge, but the image of a bookish youth keenly responsive to the delights of the natural world and the beauty of holiness was only part of the complex and even tempestuous character that was now beginning to form. His schoolfellows were certainly aware of this. While they sometimes considered him 'Welsh and mad', the purveyor of endless stories about knights and fairies, they also recalled him as '. . . a thick-set, strong-looking boy, with a high colour and . . . curly hair, good-natured and kind, but with a fearful temper'.

That temper was never to leave him (it was, perhaps, epileptic in its origins) and was an essential part of Morris's immense vitality, a physical restlessness that made his hands ache to be busy. In these early schoolboy days, the compulsion was satisfied by endless netting, and a friend described how: '. . . with one end of the net fastened to a desk in the big school-room he would work at it for hours together, his fingers moving almost mechanically.'

The rebel, too, was beginning to form. If Morris took no part in the disturbances at Marlborough which eventually caused his mother to withdraw him from the school and place him under a private tutor, at the end of his life Morris was explicit about relating his deep instinct for rebellion to his childhood. In an undated letter eventually published in the *Labour Leader*, he saw his earliest years as the origin of those emotional forces that were to make him a founder of the socialist movement. 'My parents did as all right people do,' he wrote, 'shook off the responsibility of my education as soon as they could; handing me over first to nurses, then to grooms and gardeners, and then to a school – a boy farm, I should say. In one way or another I learned chiefly one thing from all these – rebellion.'

It was an attitude that was to continue through his adolescence, though at this stage it still took the somewhat haughty form of an exclusive High Church enthusiasm. Morris's deepening perception of the beautiful and the true – his utter contempt for the sordid commercialism of his age – were beginning to be deeply rooted however. When, at the age of seventeen, his mother brought him to the Great Exhibition, he is said to have sat down and refused to go inside because he had heard that the exhibits themselves were 'wonderfully ugly'.

Morris was thus opposing himself to much that his society most cherished: the complacent materialism of Victorian values. Though it was to take many forms and many years fully to mature, that opposition was to shape Morris's life and be the foundation of the staggering range of his achievements.

THE BROTHERHOOD

In 1852, Morris sat the matriculation exam to Exeter College, Oxford. When he went up the following year, new friends and the ancient city were to widen his ideas, deepen his opposition to the materialism of the age and begin to clarify his sense of mission.

It was in Oxford that Morris first met the closest of his lifelong friends, the son of a poor Birmingham picture-framer who was later to make his reputation as the painter Edward Burne-Jones. Their friendship was immediate. Burne-Jones in particular was drawn to Morris's energy and vehement conversation and to those periods of shared reflection and reverie they indulged as they wandered through the grey and yellow stone streets, breathing in the spirit of the Middle Ages from the buildings of Merton and the cloisters of New College especially.

Friends at Pembroke were soon to join them: Charles Faulkner, the mathematician who was later to be so involved in Morris's business concerns; R.W. Dixon, the minor religious poet; William Fulford, and Cormell Price, known as 'Crom', and later to distinguish himself as a headmaster. A group of fine spirits, they felt themselves called, in the words of Burne-Jones, to a 'Crusade and Holy Warfare against the age'. Eventually, they united themselves under the name of 'The Brotherhood'.

For all of these young men, something of the Anglo-Catholic fires of the Oxford Movement still burned in the city, and both Morris and Burne-Jones regarded themselves at this stage as destined for the Church. Though the reception of Cardinal Newman into the Roman fold had been a profound shock to the Movement – and a blow to the Anglican community from which it was still reeling many years later – the values that had originally been prized still made up one form of opposition to the crass commercialism of the age.

Through his *Tracts*, Newman's luminous intellect, his absolute and instinctive devotion to a religion which seemed to satisfy men's deepest spiritual needs, had stirred a generation. The complacent superiority of conventional Protestantism was severely dented, and large sections of the Anglican Church had been

Above: *John Ruskin's drawing of St Mary's church and All Souls' College, Oxford deftly suggests the medieval character of the city that was so to inspire Morris.*

Opposite: The Return of the Dove to the Ark *was painted by John Everett Millais in 1851. It was purchased by Thomas Coombe, Printer to the University of Oxford, and it was there that Morris saw the work that was to kindle his enthusiasm for the Pre-Raphaelite movement.*

forced to recognise their insular philistinism. Together – and often with Morris reading aloud – both he and Burne-Jones immersed themselves in High Church theology. The sense of mission ran deep but had not yet found its true course. Meanwhile, vigorous fencing practice (Morris ran up exceptional bills for broken swordsticks) and the more relaxed pleasures of boating helped to work off Morris's vitality.

Long periods in the Bodleian Library also won him to the beauties of medieval manuscript illumination. The novels of Charles Kingsley introduced him to the ideals of Christian Socialism, while *The Heir of Redclyffe* by Charlotte Young gave him an image of the chivalric medieval knight transposed into the sordid world of modern commercialism. It was now that Morris was also to come in contact with the work of the two contemporary thinkers who were profoundly to shape the direction of his thought and to show him the true significance of the medieval: Carlyle and Ruskin.

Right: *Millais' portrait of John Ruskin was painted on a fateful holiday in 1854 when the painter fell in love with the critic's wife. Ruskin was to open Morris's mind and eyes to the wonders of Gothic art as well as to the grim exploitation that underlay the contemporary world.*

There was hardly an English intellectual in the 1840s and '50s who was not affected by the writings of Carlyle. In an age that tended to formulate its problems in religious terms but was often dissatisfied with the conventional forms of religion itself, Carlyle spoke as a prophet who was at once moral and romantic. He fulfilled his own ideal of the hero: the man of spiritual insight in a society of the blind who all good men would recognise and follow. It was not Carlyle's logic that convinced however but the imaginative power with which he revealed the maladies of the age. In 'Signs of the Times', for example, he voiced the feelings of those appalled by the culture that had produced the Great Exhibition:

> Men are grown mechanical in head and in heart, as well as in hand. They have lost faith in individual endeavour, and in natural force, of any kind. Not for internal perfection, but for external combinations and arrangements, for institutions, constitutions – for Mechanism of one sort or another, do they hope and struggle.

The social anguish this inflicted on the poor both revolted and frightened Carlyle, and it was he who first raised 'the Condition of England Question' and pointed out the dehumanising effects of what he called 'the cash nexus'. In *Past and Present*, he rounded on the ruling classes for their failure to be responsible for the people (it never occurred to him that they might be responsible 'to' the people) and divided the rich into dilettante aristocrats and vulgar bourgeois 'Mammonists'.

Carlyle also analysed the effects of the Industrial Revolution with exceptional insight and urged reform, social responsibility and social cohesion. Finally, he used his prodigious historical reading to draw a powerful contrast between nineteenth century Britain and the England of the Middle Ages, between a society of materialism and strife and an imagined world of order, instinctive respect for superiors and true moral leadership. In such a society, a man could properly fulfil himself through what for Carlyle was his most human quality: his work.

An image of the social and spiritual well-being of the Middle Ages was also central to the thinking of another and finer critic, John Ruskin. When the second volume of *The Stones of Venice* and its great chapter on 'The Nature of Gothic' appeared in 1853, The Brotherhood discovered their sacred text. To Morris, reciting the book's set-piece passages to his Oxford friends, Ruskin was the master who both formulated his deepest discontents and gave voice to his sense of mission. When, at the end of his career, Morris printed an edition of Ruskin's 'The Nature of Gothic', he described it as '. . . one of the very few necessary and inevitable utterances of the century'.

Ruskin's greatness as a critic lay in his profound understanding of the relationship between art and the society that produces it. His extraordinary visual responsiveness was also matched by an exceptional gift for word-painting—*The Stones of Venice* taught Morris and his generation to see—while the alliance of these powers with a crusading sense of social crisis also taught them to think.

Below: *Ford Maddox Brown's* Work *(1852–65) sums up much of the ethos praised by the intellectual Thomas Carlyle, shown on the right of the canvas with F. D. Maurice. Other figures represent beggary, wealth and manual labour.*

Ruskin's The Nature of Gothic *is one of his most passionately and coherently argued pieces of prose. It is an angry defiance of the horrors of Victorian industrialisation. The work was to influence Morris profoundly.*

You must either make a tool of the creature, or a man of him. You cannot make both. Men were not intended to work with the accuracy of tools, to be precise and perfect in all their actions. If you will have that precision out of them, and make their fingers measure degrees like cog-wheels, and their arms strike curves like compasses, you must unhumanize them. All the energy of their spirits must be given to make cogs and compasses of themselves. All their attention and strength must go to the accomplishment of the mean act. The eye of the soul must be bent upon the finger-point, and the soul's force must fill all the invisible nerves that guide it, ten hours a day, that it may not err from its steely precision, and so soul and sight be worn away, and the whole human being be lost at last—a heap of sawdust, so far as its intellectual work in this world is concerned: saved only by its Heart, which cannot go into the form of cogs and compasses, but expands, after the ten hours are over, into fireside humanity. On the other hand, if you will make a man of the working creature, you cannot make a tool. Let him but begin to imagine, to think, to try to do anything worth doing; and the engine-turned precision is lost at once. Out come all his roughness, all his dulness, all his incapability; shame upon shame, failure upon failure, pause after pause: but out comes the whole majesty of him also; and we know the height of it only when we see the clouds settling upon him. And, whether the clouds be bright or dark, there will be transfiguration behind and within them.

And now, reader, look around this English room of yours, about which you have been proud so often, because the work of it was so good and strong, and the ornaments of it so finished. Examine again all those accurate mouldings, and perfect polishings, and unerring adjustments of the seasoned wood and tempered steel. Many a time you have exulted over them, and thought how great England was, because her slightest work was done so thoroughly. Alas! if read rightly, these perfectnesses are signs of a slavery in our England a thousand times more bitter and more degrading than that of the scourged African, or helot Greek. Men may be beaten, tormented, yoked like cattle, slaughtered like summer flies, and yet remain in one sense, and the best sense, free. But to smother their souls with them, to blight and hew into rotting pollards the suckling branches of their human intelligence, to make the flesh and skin which, after the worm's work on it, is to see God, into leathern thongs to yoke machinery with,—this is to be slave-masters indeed; and there might be more freedom in England, though her feudal lords' lightest words were worth men's lives, and though the blood of the vexed husbandman dropped in the furrows of her fields, than there is while the animation of her multitudes is sent like fuel to feed the factory smoke, and the strength of them is given daily to be wasted into the fineness of a web, or racked into the exactness of a line.

In this passage from The Nature of Gothic, *Ruskin asks the Victorian reader to look at the sumptuous furnishings of his house and to view them not as a triumph of modern progress but as the expression of industrial slavery.*

Ruskin's work showed Morris how art is a public concern, a measure of a nation's well-being rather than merely a hobby for the elite. A decline in artistic standards – the vulgarity of the objects in the Great Exhibition, for example – was an image of a deep cultural malaise. For Ruskin, this proceeded from the triumph of the machine, from the division of labour and the reduction of the worker to a cog in the great engine of commerce:

an engine that churned out spiritually dead artifacts for a society where the malignant Goddess of Getting-on had reduced man to '. . . ennui, and jaded intellect, and uncomfortableness of soul and body'.

Against this warping of the spirit Ruskin juxtaposed the values he saw enshrined in Gothic art. To a young man like Morris with his love of the medieval and his deep, instinctive revulsion at the items in the Crystal Palace, a young man who detected, however imprecisely, the spiritual bondage and corruption that produced what Ruskin described as '. . . all those accurate mouldings, and perfect polishings, and unerring adjustments of the seasoned wood and the tempered steel,' *The Stones of Venice* was a profound inspiration.

In the art of the Middle Ages Ruskin saw an expression of man's delight in his labour which was to become the foundation of Morris's beliefs.

And, on the other hand, go forth again to gaze upon the old cathedral front, where you have smiled so often at the fantastic ignorance of the old sculptors: examine once more those ugly goblins, and formless monsters, and stern statues, anatomiless and rigid; but do not mock at them, for they are signs of the life and liberty of every workman who struck the stone; a freedom of thought, and rank in scale of being, such as no laws, no charters, no charities can secure; but which it must be the first aim of all Europe at this day to regain for her children.

Ruskin here describes the spiritual torment inflicted on people by the horrors of industrialism and the division of labour.

We have much studied and much perfected, of late, the great civilized invention of the division of labour; only we give it a false name. It is not, truly speaking, the labour that is divided; but the men:—Divided into mere segments of men—broken into small fragments and crumbs of life; so that all the little piece of intelligence that is left in a man is not enough to make a pin, or a nail, but exhausts itself in making the point of a pin or the head of a nail. Now it is a good and desirable thing, truly, to make many pins in a day; but if we could only see with what crystal sand their points were polished,—sand of human soul, much to be magnified before it can be discerned for what it is—we should think there might be some loss in it also. And the great cry that rises from all our manufacturing cities, louder than their furnace blast, is all in very deed for this,—that we manufacture everything there except men. . . .

Ruskin saw that the division of labour also led to a corroding division in society.

We are always in these days endeavouring to separate the two; we want one man to be always thinking, and another to be always working, and we call one a gentleman, and the other an

operative; whereas the workman ought often to be thinking, and
the thinker often to be working, and both should be gentlemen, in
the best sense. As it is, we make both ungentle, the one envying,
the other despising, his brother; and the mass of society is made
up of morbid thinkers, and miserable workers. Now it is only by
labour that thought can be made healthy, and only by thought
that labour can be made happy, and the two cannot be separated
with impunity. It would be well if all of us were good
handicraftsmen in some kind, and the dishonour of manual
labour done away with altogether. . . .

Now, in the medieval beauty of Oxford, Morris had all around
him examples of that Gothic architecture which for Ruskin
expressed man's soul at its most fully human. In place of the inert,
the repetitious and the flashily vulgar were the Gothic virtues that
accepted man's imperfection and irregularity as essential parts of
his nature. Here was an art that saw ornament as an expression of
the worker's delight in his craft rather than a sumptuous excres-
cence that pandered to the vanity of the purchaser. Here, instead
of dull order was perpetual novelty, freedom and exuberance. In
Merton and New College, Morris was surrounded by an architecture which could, in Ruskin's words: '. . . shrink into a turret,
expand into a hall, coil into a staircase, or spring into a spire, with
undegraded grace and unexhausted energy.' Gothic was a form of
art that was natural, human and beautiful, an art which expressed
a social world of '. . . tranquil and gentle existence, sustained by
the gifts, and gladdened by the splendour, of the earth'. The love
of history and the love of the natural world were here fused in a
love of the nature of man himself.

Such an ideal was a vantage-point from which to survey the
social degradation of the modern world of commerce. 'The
Nature of Gothic' is eloquent with a hatred of all that the young
Morris himself despised. Above all, it taught him to understand
that it is not a sufficient response merely to turn one's back on
such things, to sit down and pointedly refuse to enter the Crystal
Palace. The deepest wrong was not vulgarity itself but the society
that produced it, and it was against this a man should struggle.

The impact of such ideas was profoundly exciting but it was
also to take some time fully to mature. Meanwhile, and with
Ruskin's works as a guide, Morris made his first expedition to
some of the great continental centres of medieval art.

In Paris he visited the Musée de Cluny with its sumptuous collections of medieval tapestry and Gothic furniture. In Amiens,
Beauvais, Rouen and Chartres the full splendour of Gothic architecture was revealed to him with unforgettable pleasure. In the

little towns and cities of Belgium he saw the work of the great medieval painters, Memling and Van Eyck. It was an experience of quite exceptional imaginative enrichment, for here were the works on which Morris was to draw throughout a lifetime. It was a world of colour, texture and superb design, of tapestries woven with wools of natural dye, of furniture true to the natural qualities of oak, of buildings at once fantastic and serene, and of painters whose work glowed with a radiance of pigment and spirituality unmatched by any of the masters of Ruskin's much despised Italian renaissance.

But who was creating such work now? Once again, it was Ruskin who, in his Edinburgh Lectures, pointed the way. Burne-Jones provides the most vivid picture of the excited young Morris's response. 'I was reading in my room,' Burne-Jones recalled, 'when Morris ran in one morning bringing the newly published book with him: so everything was put aside until he read it all through to me. And there we first saw about the Pre-Raphaelites, and there I first saw the name of Rossetti.'

Right: *Hans Memlinc's* Virgin and Child with Sir John Donne and Family *was painted in the 1460s. The gorgeous fabrics of the attendant saints and angels are beautifully rendered, while the hanging behind the Virgin's throne is based on a sinuous motif similar to that Morris was to use in some of his own late fabrics. Beyond the figures is a soft and radiant landscape perfectly blended with the works of man. The picture thus portrays two of Morris's principal loves: the art of the middle ages and the loveliness of the unspoiled countryside.*

The Pre-Raphaelite Brotherhood had been founded in 1848 as a secret society of those young artists disaffected with the long traditional schooling offered by the Royal Academy. Its principal figures were John Everett Millais, William Holman Hunt, and the erratic genius who was to play so central and bitter a role in Morris's life, Dante Gabriel Rossetti. Each was influenced by the religious passion and factual truthfulness, the angularity and shallow recession of those Italian painters who worked before the dominance of what Ruskin called 'the clear and tasteless poison of the art of Raphael'.

Just as Ruskin himself in his own very able drawings and watercolours had learned to eschew conventional pictorial devices for a vivid concern with the minutiae of the natural world, so the Pre-Raphaelites united truth to nature with a conscious archaism of design, with literary allusion and emblematic detail. Technically, they made a radical stand against the much-admired dark tones of the accepted old masters, a darkness increased by the use of bitumen which continues to blacken over the course of

Above: *Dante Gabriel Rossetti executed this self-portrait in 1855, the year before Morris met him and fell under his spell.*

time. For these older practices, the Pre-Raphaelites substituted a carefully prepared wet white ground laid over a preparatory drawing. They then meticulously built up their detail through small brushstrokes loaded with brilliant colour.

Again, just as their technique was in revolt against the established ideas, so too in their religious works especially they opposed the norms of the High Renaissance by their attempt to democratise rather than ennoble their subjects. Their use of contemporary and Romantic poets also shows them in revolt against the commercialism of the age. Tennyson offered them a world beautified by reminiscences of chivalry and the ideals of art, while poems such as Keats's *Isabella* and *The Eve of Saint Agnes* portrayed an existence in which the imagination defied the corrupt and mundane.

At first the work of the Pre-Raphaelites was well-received, but with the publication of their short-lived magazine *The Germ* – important as the first English journal of an avant-garde artistic group – the existence of a quasi-secret society of painters dedicated to the overthrow of traditional standards roused the opposition of the press.

Critics objected to their refusal to subordinate detail to a central, dramatically lit subject, while the chief figure in Millais' *Christ in the House of his Parents* was jeered at by Dickens for showing '. . . a hideous, wry-necked, blubbering, red-haired boy in a nightgown'. For Ruskin however, this very fidelity to nature was the great strength of the school. 'Pre-Raphaelitism has but one principle,' he declared, 'that of absolute, uncompromising truth in all that it does, obtained by working everything, down to the most minute detail, from nature only.'

Millais in particular continued to develop this approach, and in 1851 he submitted to the Royal Academy exhibition three pictures including *The Return of the Dove to the Ark*. This is an example of Pre-Raphaelite painting at its most direct and appealing. It was also a picture that Ruskin himself wished to buy and the work which first caused him to come to the defence of the Pre-Raphaelites themselves. The canvas had already been purchased however by Thomas Combe, Printer to the University of Oxford. Eventually, the painting was put on display in Oxford, and it was there that Morris had his first glimpse of the work of the movement that was so profoundly to influence him.

By now, Morris's reading, his travels and friendships, his vigorous discussions and the innate abilities that were being so stimulated by the new experiences he was exposing himself to, were greatly broadening his mind. Just as at school he had largely conducted his own education, so at Oxford it was his personal discoveries rather than a formal course of study that were laying the foundations of his future achievements.

His friends were certainly becoming aware of his growing stature. 'How Morris seems to know things, doesn't he?' Faulkner observed to Dixon. Dixon was struck by the truth of the remark. 'I observed how decisive he was: how accurate, without any effort or formality: what extraordinary power of observation lay at the base of many of his casual or incidental remarks, and how many things he knew that were quite out of our way.'

Nothing pleased and excited them more than to discover that Morris was a poet. In fact, their praise was largely the admiration of an enthusiastic young clique for one of its members, since these early verses (which Morris chose later not to print) show little more than a talent for imitation and versifying. The latter was a gift that was never to leave him however and, in some of the most troubled periods of his life, was to be a source of great solace. Morris himself nonetheless was aware of the danger of his facility. 'If this is poetry,' he declared, 'it is very easy to write.'

The first fruits of Morris's interest in prose romance also date from this period. There are seven of these, and some of the most successful such as 'Lindenberg Pool' show how early Morris was interested in the Nordic themes that were to occupy much of his middle years, an interest initially inspired by his reading of Benjamin Thorpe's *Northern Mythology*. Some of the most successful tales also show a strong interest in the emotional crises of love, but the best of them, 'The Story of the Unknown Church', contains a number of other suggestive themes: the deep need for friendship and a life devoted to art, a feeling for how the world ought to be made beautiful for people to live in and, above all, a delight in flowers and nature that is at once sensuous, detailed and deeply responsive to colour, shape and variety. The love of tendril and leaf, of intertwining forms and colours that Morris had acquired as a boy and which was to be the inspiration of some of his finest designs, was always available to him as a source of joy.

In the garden were trellises covered over with roses, and convolvulus, and the great-leaved fiery nasturtium; and specially all along by the poplar trees were there trellises, but on these grew nothing but deep crimson roses; the hollyhocks too were all out in blossom at that time, great spires of pink, and orange, and red, and white, with their soft, downy leaves. I said that nothing grew on the trellises by the poplars but crimson roses, but I was not quite right, for in many places the wild flowers had crept into the garden from without; lush green briony, with green-white blossoms, that grows so fast, one could almost think that we see it grow, and deadly nightshade, La bella donna, O! so beautiful; red berry, and purple, yellow-spiked flower, and deadly, cruel-

This passage from Morris's 'The Story of the Unknown Church' suggests his deep and detailed love of nature. Such feelings were later to inspire some of his finest designs.

looking, dark green leaf, all growing together in the glorious days of early autumn.

Considerable financial resources were now also to hand. When Morris came of age in March 1885, he inherited £900 a year. Comparative wealth meant liberty and perhaps the greatest freedom of all – the freedom to choose his work.

One project he started was *The Oxford and Cambridge Magazine* in which he and the other members of The Brotherhood could publish their writings. The journal lasted for a year, mostly due to the editorial efforts of William Fulford. In addition to Morris's own poems and stories, it published a range of critical essays on Ruskin, Tennyson, Browning and Thackeray, on Mrs Gaskell and Charlotte Brontë, on the position of women and the duty of modern young men to give deep consideration to '... social wrongs, their causes, and the best way in which they, each in their several spheres, may help to heal them'. Rossetti published three poems in later editions, and both Ruskin and Tennyson were warm in their praise.

More decisive was a second visit to France Morris made with Burne-Jones and Fulford. Once again, it was Gothic architecture

Below: *Rossetti's* Dante Drawing an Angel on the Anniversary of the Death of Beatrice *is an exquisite watercolour in the Pre-Raphaelite manner executed in 1853. Its combination of the visual and poetic arts is suggestive of the interests of the entire movement and of Morris himself.*

that made the greatest impression on him. Amiens cathedral excited 'intense exultation' as did Mont St Michel. Modern restoration however – the clumsy, spiritless zeal for imposing a spurious unity on old buildings – roused the anger that later in his life was to move Morris to lead one of his most important campaigns: the founding of the Society for the Preservation of Ancient Buildings.

I think I felt inclined to shout when I first entered Amiens Cathedral. It is so free and vast and noble that I did not feel the least awestruck or humbled by its size and grandeur: I have not often felt thus when looking on architecture, but have felt at all events at first, intense exultation at the beauty of it. That, and a certain kind of satisfaction in looking at the geometrical tracery of the windows, and the sweep of the huge arches, were I think my first feelings in Amiens Cathedral.

Morris describes the effect of medieval architecture on him.

To offset such modern errors and the horror of the new railways, there was the beauty of the French countryside. The fields in particular delighted Morris and he described their loveliness '. . . mingled with the flowers, purple thistles, and blue cornflowers, and red poppies, growing together with corn round the roots of the fruit trees . . . as if they had always grown there, without change of seasons, knowing no other time than early August'.

It was on the quay at Le Havre, late on one of these August nights, and with the memory of a score of churches still fresh in their minds, that for both Morris and Burne-Jones there came a moment of profound decision and commitment. The young men who had gone up to Oxford to study for the Church now realised that their vocations lay elsewhere. They would not take Holy Orders but devote their lives to art: Jones as a painter, Morris as an architect. Their interests and sense of mission, their excited conversation over the past year, had brought them to this point '. . . and after that night's talk we never hesitated more'.

How deeply this decision affected Morris is best told in the words of J.W. Mackail, his first biographer. 'For him, then and always, the word architecture bore an immense, and one might say a transcendental, meaning. Connected at a thousand points with all the other specific arts which ministered to it out of a thousand sources, it was itself the tangible expression of all the order, the comeliness, the sweetness, nay, even the mystery and the law, which sustain man's world and make human life what it is.' For Morris to commit himself to architecture was to commit himself to an ideal of existence made better and more beautiful through the exercise of art.

Returning to England, and while reading for his finals, Morris wrote to George Street of Oxford – one of the most original architects of the Gothic revival – asking to enter his office. He firmly brushed aside the objections of his mother, and in letters to his friends suggested the personal importance of his decision as well as the need for haste and purpose if he were not to be '. . . a lazy, aimless, useless, dreamy body all my life long'.

Morris's letter to his mother in which he told her that he was not going to enter holy orders but to take up the life of an artist shows the force with which he could argue his position.

I am almost afraid you thought me scarcely in earnest when I told you a month or two ago that I did not intend taking Holy Orders; if this is the case I am afraid also that my letter now may vex you; but if you really have made up your mind that I was in earnest I should hope you will be well pleased with my resolution. You said then, you remember, and said very truly, that it was an evil thing to be an idle, objectless man; I am fully determined not to incur this reproach, I was so then though I did not tell you at the time all I thought of . . . partly because I had not thought about it enough myself, and partly because I wished to give you time to become reconciled to the idea of my continuing a lay person. I wish now to be an architect, an occupation I have often had a hankering after, even during the time when I intended taking Holy Orders; the signs of which hankerings you yourself have doubtless often seen.

If I were not to follow this occupation I in truth know not what I should follow with any chance of success, or hope of happiness in my work, in this I am pretty confident I shall succeed, and make I hope a decent architect sooner or later; and you know too that in any work one delights in, even the merest drudgery connected with it is delightful too—I shall be master too of a useful trade, one by which I should hope to earn money, not altogether precariously, if other things fail . . . it will be rather grievous to my pride and self-will to have to do just as I am told for three long years, but good for it too I think . . . Perhaps you think that people will laugh at me, and call me purposeless and changeable; I have no doubt they will, but I in my turn will try to shame them, God being my helper, by steadiness and hard work.

. . . I do not hope to be great at all in anything, but perhaps I may reasonably hope to be happy in my work, and sometimes when I am idle and doing nothing, pleasant visions go past me of the things that may be.

On 21 January 1856 Morris signed his articles and was introduced into the happy office of an architect whose sumptuous polychromatic church interiors are fine examples of Victorian High Gothic taste and whose interest in a range of arts – in painting, fabrics, stained glass and wrought iron – suggests that mastery of several skills which was to be profoundly influential on two of his most brilliant pupils: Morris himself and Philip Webb who was soon to become a close friend.

Burne-Jones, meanwhile, had gone to London to learn painting under the tutelage of Rossetti. Morris spent most weekends in their company, and the power of Rossetti's personality exerted an ever stronger attraction for him. Through his study of Dante and his love affair with Lizzie Siddal, Rossetti had developed his own distinctive style within the Pre-Raphaelite movement. His love of Malory was also sympathetic to the young men, and when he told Morris, 'If a man had any poetry in him he should paint, for it has all been said and written, and they have hardly begun to paint it,' Morris was won over.

Perhaps, after all, architecture was not his true vocation. For nine months – and in addition to experiments in sculpture, manuscript illumination and embroidery design – Morris had laboured over a drawing of the doorway of St Augustine's Church, Canterbury, working at it until his compass point nearly dug a hole in his drawing board. Painting and bohemia began to seem more attractive, and in November 1856 Morris and Burne-Jones moved into 17 Red Lion Square, the rooms once occupied by their new master Rossetti.

If there was a strong element of escapism in all this – a flight from the social commitment of his undergraduate days – Morris was fully aware of it. 'I can't enter into politico-social subjects with any interest,' he wrote to Cormell Price, 'for on the whole I see that things are in a muddle, and I have no power or vocation to set them right in ever so little a degree. My work is the embodiment of dreams in one form or another.' This was to be true of his whole life, but very slowly, and through years of astonishing productivity, such dreams were to mature into a vision of matchless optimism for the future of mankind. Meanwhile, Morris had to continue his apprenticeship.

APPRENTICESHIP AND MARRIAGE

Morris began to wear his hair long and ceased to shave his beard. The bohemian camaraderie of Red Lion Square suited his ebullient personality, though his bursts of anger were still common. These may in part have resulted from the hard and troublesome labour he was now putting into his painting, particularly the practice of figure-drawing which he frankly detested. 'He brooded much by himself, and lost for a time a good deal of his old sweetness and affectionateness of manner,' Mackail recorded. Clearly, Morris's intense nervous energy was being severely tested, and to this was no doubt added the debilitating realisation that he did not have a first rate aptitude for the subject in which he wished to shine. He had given up architecture after nine months. Would it be the same with painting?

But if there was self-doubt, there was also warmth, friendship and success in unexpected areas. It is from this period that Morris's work as a decorator begins.

He and Burne-Jones needed to furnish their rooms but were unable easily to buy tables and chairs which were in the least suitable. The reasons for this throw an interesting light on the world of commercial decoration that Morris was soon to help so decisively to transform.

By the 1850s, large furniture retailers found they could cut their expenses and raise their profits by ceasing to keep journeymen cabinetmakers and buying their stock piecemeal from 'garretmasters'. These were small, independent men, sometimes assisted by their wives and children, whose meagre livelihoods depended on a quick turnover. As a result of these purely commercial pressures, real quality suffered. The garretmasters could not afford to maintain it, the retailers apparently did not require it. 'Make an inferior article so it's cheap,' the social observer Mayhew reports one retailer as having said to a garretmaster, 'If it comes to pieces in a month, what's that to you or me?'

The inevitable result was 'scamping', the production of shoddy goods artfully disguised. Nothing was more helpful here than veneers. The highly respected skill of cutting veneers by hand had now been replaced by a machine which could cut the original

Opposite: *D. G. Rossetti created a number of pictures such as* The Blue Closet *which were closely inspired by Morris's poems.*

timber more thinly, faster and cheaper. To the hard-pressed garretmaster, these new veneers were a boon, and the scamping hand soon learned their use. Cheap deal covered with cheap veneer easily made a gaudily acceptable piece of furniture—a lady's sewing-box, for example. 'Such boxes are nailed together,' one garretmaster told Mayhew. 'There's no dove-tailing, nothing what I call *work* or workmanship, as you say about them, but the deal's nailed together, and the veneer's dabbed on, and if the deal's covered, why the thing passes'.

The vulgarity and solemn ordinariness of most expensive furniture and the gimcrack quality of the rest left Morris little choice but to design his own and supervise its manufacture. Hence the famous 'great settle' that was eventually installed in Red Lion Square and reportedly filled a third of the studio. A table 'as firm and heavy as a rock' followed along with chairs fit for a medieval emperor. Rossetti thoroughly approved even if he was mildly amused, and instead of cheap veneer and polish he painted the panels on the settle with scenes from Dante and Morris's poems. The furniture was a protest, an assertion of quality over commercialism, and an experiment that was to be extremely fruitful.

Right: *Max Beerbohm's cartoon portrays 'Topsy and Ned settled on the Settle in Red Lion Square.' 'Topsy' was the nickname by which Morris was known through much of his life. 'Ned' is Edward Burne-Jones. The enormous settle itself was made by Morris for their lodgings and was decorated by Rosetti with figures from Morris's poems.*

Another well-known episode also dates from this period, though its practical results were to be far from lasting. This was the project to fresco the bays in the gallery of the Oxford Union debating chamber with ten scenes from Malory's *Morte d'Arthur*.

The original idea was Rossetti's and it was he who persuaded the architect Benjamin Woodward to give him and his friends access to the building. They would donate their work while the Union would bear the cost of lodging and materials. It was all an affair of the happiest midsummer madness. 'What fun we had! What jokes! What roars of laughter!' remembered Val Prinsep, a sensitive young man who, though he protested his inexperience of painting, was encouraged to come along by Rossetti who told him that Morris was in the same position but would undoubtedly do 'something very good'.

I found Rossetti in a plum-coloured frockcoat, and a short square man with spectacles and a vast mop of dark hair. I was cordially received. 'Top', cried Rossetti, 'let me introduce Val Prinsep.'

'Glad, I'm sure,' answered the man in spectacles, nodding his head, and then he resumed his reading of a large quarto. This was William Morris. Soon after, the door opened, and before it was half opened in glided Burne-Jones. 'Ned,' said Rossetti, who had been absently humming to himself, 'I think you know Prinsep.' The shy figure darted forward, the shy face lit up, and I was received with the kindly effusion which was natural to him.

When dinner was over, Rossetti, humming to himself as was his wont, rose from the table and proceeded to curl himself up on the sofa. 'Top,' he said, 'read us one of your grinds.' 'No, Gabriel,' answered Morris, 'you have heard them all.' 'Never mind,' said Rossetti, 'here's Prinsep who has never heard them, and besides, they are devilish good.' 'Very well, old chap,' growled Morris, and having got his book he began to read in a sing-song chant some of the poems afterwards published in his first volume. All the time, he was jigging about nervously with his watch chain. I was then a very young man and my experience of life was therefore limited, but the effect produced on my mind was so strong that to this day, forty years after, I can still recall the scene: Rossetti on the sofa with large melancholy eyes fixed on Morris, the poet at the table reading and ever fidgetting with his watch chain, and Burne-Jones working at a pen-and-ink drawing.

> Gold on her head, and gold on her feet,
> And gold where the hems of her kirtle
>   meet,
> And a golden girdle round my sweet;
>   Ah! qu'elle est belle La Marguerite

still seems to haunt me, and this other stanza:

> Swerve to left, son Roger, he said,
> When you catch his eyes through the helmet slit

Val Prinsep describes an evening spent with Morris, Rossetti, Burne-Jones at the time they were painting the walls of the Oxford Union debating chamber.

Swerve to the left, then out at his head,
And the Lord God give you joy of it!

I confess I returned to the Mitre with my brain in a whirl.

Amid laughter and the pop of soda bottles, modelling for each other and delighting in the armour that Morris had had specially made for them to copy, the young men set to work, largely ignorant of fresco technique. The newly built walls of the Union were still wet and the only ground used was a coat of whitewash. The paint sank in or flaked off, and Lancelot's vision of the Sangreal was as evanescent as in Malory's tale. After a mere six months, all that remained of Morris's fresco was its profusion of sunflowers and the head of Sir Tristram.

Since he was the first to finish however, Morris turned his attention elsewhere and began to paint the ceiling with a pattern of flowers and foliage. It was, recalled Burne-Jones '. . . a wonder to us for its originality and fitness, for he had never before designed anything of the kind'. Here was proof of Morris's real talent, and though Morris himself repainted his work in 1875, the original was a decorative scheme of the greatest import.

Throughout that summer, the influence of Rossetti was felt by all the young men. 'He was the planet round which we all revolved,' Prinsep recalled. They sank their individuality in the strong personality of their 'adored Gabriel', copying his mannerisms and tricks of speech and calling every beautiful woman a 'Stunner'.

One such young woman was Jane Burden, the daughter of a ostler at the Holywell stables and a figure of legendary beauty. Henry James's description of her, though written twelve years after Jane's introduction to the young painters in the Union, cannot be surpassed for the subtlety of its rapturous analysis:

A figure cut out of a missal—one of Rossetti's or Hunt's pictures—to say this gives but a faint idea of her, because when such a shape puts on flesh and blood, it is an apparition of fearful and wonderful intensity. It's hard to say whether she's a grand synthesis of all the Pre-Raphaelite pictures ever made—or they a 'keen analysis' of her—whether she's an original or a copy. In either case she is a wonder. Imagine a tall lean woman in a long dress of some dead purple stuff, guiltless of hoops (or of anything else, I should say), with a mass of crisp black hair heaped into great wavy projections on each side of her temples, a thin pale face, a pair of strange, sad, deep, dark, Swinburnian eyes, with great thick black oblique brows, joined in the middle and tucking

Left: *The project to decorate the interior of the Oxford Union was one of the early highpoints in Morris's career. Though the scenes themselves rapidly faded because of inadequate preparation, Morris's work on the ceiling revealed his great skills as a decorator.*

themselves away under her hair, a mouth like the 'Oriana' in our illustrated Tennyson, a long neck, without any collar, and in lieu thereof some dozen strings of outlandish beads.

The description penetrates to the core of the problem: Jane is both a creation of Pre-Raphaelite art and its inspiration. She is the source and embodiment of dreams. This makes it difficult for us to glimpse the real woman, yet the confusion of fact with fantasy is central to the private anguish of Morris's later life.

Jane was Rossetti's discovery. It was he who first saw the power of her unconventional beauty and it is clear that she was also attracted to him. She was then nearly eighteen. Charity schools had given her a basic education in domestic skills (she was later to prove herself a formidable needlewoman) yet her prospects must have seemed at best limited. With little to lose and much to gain, intelligent and shrewd, her introduction to a lively group of socially superior young men was an irresistible opportunity.

At first she sat chiefly to Rossetti, probably for a fee, and her dark image began to replace Lizzie Siddal's in his drawings of this time. She becomes Guenevere in *Lancelot in the Queen's Chamber* and the princess in *The Wedding of Saint George*. But if Rossetti found in Jane a new source of inspiration, he was still tied by duties to his earlier muse. Lizzie Sidall summoned him to Matlock where she was to spend the winter and to face the tragic realisation that her relationship with Rossetti was effectively at an end.

For Jane, the sudden loss of Rossetti and the hard truth that another woman appeared to have greater power over him than she, must have appeared as a dreadful blow to her hopes. To lose contact with the young painters in the Union was to lose her chance of being anything more than a serving girl.

She need not have worried. If the king had temporarily withdrawn from his little medieval court, his devoted squire stayed on. 'I want to imitate Gabriel as much as possible,' Morris had declared, somewhat pathetically. Now he would imitate him by a passionate abasement before the woman his master had declared to be the symbol of earthly beauty. In the world of medieval romance, Morris could be at once squire, courtly lover and—as the affair progressed towards marriage—the chivalric Saint George rescuing Jane from the social dragon of poverty.

She, for her part, was later to claim that she never truly loved her husband. Nonetheless, she could not afford to lose him. He was wealthy, he was free, he seemed honourable in his intentions. That a young man from the middle classes should seriously contemplate marriage with a girl from an Oxford backstreet was an opportunity too good to miss. Morris was, besides, all too willing to be won, even if he was entirely lacking in the romantic allure that radiated from Rossetti.

Morris was, indeed, unkempt and now getting rather plump. He could appear shy and tongue-tied on some occasions, fidgety or even explosively angry on others. Suavity and grace he was wholly without. His fantasy image of Jane nonetheless ran to great refinement. If much of their courtship passed with Morris reading loud from *Barnaby Rudge*, Jane wandered his dreams in unattainable medieval perfection.

He tried to paint her, choosing with an unconscious irony to portray her as Isolde, the unfaithful wife of Mark, king of Cornwall, and a great, tragic heroine of medieval romance. The painting—which is the only one of Morris's canvases known to survive—is often wrongly entitled *Queen Guenevere*, but the little dog curled up on the unmade bed is assuredly Malory's 'brachet' given by Tristram to Isolde and which, at the close of the tale, recognises the dying knight. This was a scene that Morris was later to represent in one of his stained glass windows.

Below: *This photograph of William Morris is the earliest known portrait of the artist and was taken in his twenty-third year.*

The painting of the picture itself proceeded with agonising slowness and the canvass was subsequently reworked by both Rossetti and Maddox-Brown. It is therefore difficult to say how far it represents Morris's own intentions. The flat, constricted figure with its ungainly head certainly suggests Morris's difficulties with the human figure—friends had rather unkindly said of another study 'he can't draw the head and don't know where the hips come'—but the oppressive draperies effectively contribute to the sense of guilty emotional withdrawal. Here indeed is a portrait of a betrothed woman whose mind is obsessed with another man. As such, it cruelly prefigures the future, but for the moment the most touching anecdote associated with the work is the frustrated note the artist sent to his sitter: 'I cannot paint you, but I love you.'

The fear and distance in that love also achieved expression in other forms. In October 1857, Morris went to Manchester to see the Art Treasures Exhibition. His eye was caught particularly by the carved ivory backs of the medieval mirrors on display, items whose intimate and feminine allure potently suggests the game of love played out by medieval courtiers. Now the game was revived and found its expression in poetry. Jane's pale beauty, large dark eyes, long neck and fingers—attributes very different to those of conventional Victorian beauty—transformed the ostler's daughter into a heroine from romance:

> My lady seems of ivory
> Forehead, straight nose, and cheeks that be
> Hallow'd a little mournfully.
> —*Beata mea Domina!*—

But what is blessed, beautiful and remote is also a source of suffering and frustrated passion. For the poet of hopeless adoration, the physical and the ethereal are cruelly separated as he feels obliged to praise the source of his sorrow:

> Her great eyes, standing far apart,
> Draw up some memory from her heart,
> And gaze out very mournfully;
> —*Beata mea Domina!*—
>
> So beautiful and kind they are,
> But most times looking out afar,
> Waiting for something, not for me.
> —*Beata mea domina!*—

This combination of romance with the bleakly inexorable facts that underlie it is one of the major strengths in the volume of his verse Morris issued in March 1858 under the title *The Defence of*

Opposite: *'I cannot paint you, but I love you.' Morris's plaintive note to Jane suggested the conflicting emotions that were working in him at this time. This is Morris's only known canvas. Ironically, it presents Jane as Isolde, the unfaithful wife of King Mark, whose passionate love for Tristan is the subject of a great medieval legend. A similar triangular relationship was to exist between Morris, Jane and Rossetti.*

Guenevere, and Other Poems. The book is, indeed, an exceptional achievement, and in its power and originality far surpasses anything Morris had yet achieved in the visual arts.

The opening lines of 'The Haystack in the Floods' reveals the power and originality that underlay Morris's early medievalism.

Had she come all the way for this,
To part at last without a kiss?
Yea, had she borne the dirt and rain
That her own eyes might see him slain
Beside the haystack in the floods?

Along the dripping leafless woods,
The stirrup touching either shoe,
She rode astride as troopers do;
With kirtle kilted to her knee,
To which the mud splash'd wretchedly;
And the wet dripp'd from every tree
Upon her head and heavy hair,
And on her eyelids broad and fair;
The tears and rain ran down her face.
By fits and starts they rode apace,
And very often was his place
Far off from her; he had to ride
Ahead, to see what might betide
When the roads cross'd; and sometimes, when
There rose a murmuring from his men,
Had to turn back with promises;
Ah me! she had but little ease;
And often for pure doubt and dread
She sobb'd, made giddy in the head
By the swift riding; while, for cold,
Her slender fingers scarce could hold
The wet reins; yea, and scarcely, too,
She felt the foot within her shoe
Against the stirrup: all for this,
To part at last without a kiss
Beside the haystack in the floods.

This is one of Morris's best lyrics in his Medieval mode.

IN PRISON

Wearily, drearily,
Half the day long,
Flap the great banners
High over the stone;
Strangely and eerily
Sounds the wind's song,
Bending the banner-poles.

While, all alone,
Watching the loophole's spark,
Lie I, with life all dark,
Feet tether'd, hands fetter'd
Fast to the stone,
The grim walls, square letter'd
With prison'd men's groan.
Still strain the banner-poles
Through the wind's song,
Westward the banner rolls
Over my wrong.

The too obvious facility of his undergraduate experiments has been disciplined. There is little here which suggests a spurious idealism or a conventionally moral point of view. In the title poem, for example, Guenevere calls her beauty to witness to her virtue, and challenges the assembled knights to dare to condemn her for the extra-marital affair of which we know she is guilty. The poem is defiant as the queen is defiant, and ten years after its publication the great Victorian aesthete Walter Pater accurately defined the effect Morris achieved when he wrote: 'The poem which gives its name to the volume is a thing tormented and awry with passion, like the body of Guenevere defending herself from the charge of adultery, and the accent falls in strange, unwonted places with the effect of a great cry.'

The involved syntax arises in part from Morris's reading of Browning, but 'King Arthur's Tomb', the companion poem in the volume, has a power which is wholly Morris's own. Exhaustion, death and guilty dream, the anguish of the queen riven by penitence and the passionate memory of 'Lancelot's red-golden hair,' are all expressed through a highly dramatic use of language:

If even I go to hell, I cannot choose
        But love you, Christ, yea, though I cannot keep
From loving Lancelot! O Christ! must I lose
        My own heart's love? See, though I cannot weep,

'Yet I am very sorry for my sin . . .'

Froissart and Malory, the two great chroniclers of chivalry and the inspiration of many poems in the volume, are here brought back to life in a manner that is both courtly and brutal. This is not a tapestry world woven to hide its readers from reality but an exploration of the erotic, the occasionally hysterical and the tragic. For conventional tastes—palates that in the following year were to be soothed by Tennyson's *Idylls of the King*—such poetry was too rough for ready appreciation. Critical notices in *The*

Athenaeum, the *Spectator*, and *The Saturday Review* were universally hostile and must have deepened Morris's sense of artistic failure.

Among the more discerning however the verses were awarded high praise, and Pater was not alone in his appreciation. Ruskin admired the volume, the young Swinburne was enthusiastic, while the literary historian George Saintsbury recalled how he '... read it straight through with an ecstasy of relish not surpassed by anything I have ever known of the kind'. Others too found that Morris had recaptured a part of the true, passionate significance of the Arthurian legends and had done so in a way they found superior to Tennyson's romantic moralisations. Morris himself had objected to Tennyson's Galahad as being 'rather a mild youth,' and while he was perfectly willing to surrender to Tennyson's languorous melancholy and pay tribute to his matchless euphony, Morris's own early works are an expression of the rebellious complexity which was one of the sources of his greatness.

The published criticisms however were a severe rebuff and for the next five years Morris was to write little verse. When he took up poetry again, he was to express himself in a very different manner and in very different circumstances.

Morris's engagement to Jane was formally announced in the spring of 1858, but it was to be a year before they were actually married. While long engagements were fairly common in Victorian England, this delay almost certainly had a practical purpose. Jane was to be educated in the skills conventionally expected of a middle-class wife. Certainly, she acquired many of those forms of behaviour which subtley and sometimes cruelly indicated differences of class in Victorian England, and she was later able to play her part as hostess to some of the most diverse and brilliant men of the age. She would also have been expected to make many of the items in her trousseau at this time, and her skill as a needlewoman no doubt served her well.

Behind all this preparation however moved the still alluring figure of Rossetti. The precise nature of their relationship at this stage is difficult to fathom, but an allegorical story written by Rossetti many years later when the couple were living with each other in Morris's house is often read as a clue to what was really happening.

Rossetti's tale 'The Cup of Cold Water' can be read as an allegorical account of the relationship between Jane, Morris and himself.

The young King of a country is hunting one day with a young Knight, his friend; when, feeling thirsty, he stops at a Forester's cottage, and the Forester's daughter brings him a cup of water to drink. Both of them are equally enamoured at once of her

unequalled beauty. The King, however, has been affianced from
boyhood to a Princess, worthy of all love, and whom he had
always believed he loved until undeceived by his new absorbing
passion; but the Knight resolved to sacrifice all other
considerations to his love, goes again to the Forester's cottage
and asks his daughter's hand. He finds the girl has fixed her
thoughts on the King, whose rank she does not know. On hearing
it she tells her suitor humbly that she must die if such be her fate,
but cannot love another. The Knight goes to the King to tell him
all and beg his help; and the two friends then come to an
explanation. Ultimately the King goes to the girl and pleads his
friend's cause, not disguising his own passion, but saying that as
he sacrificed himself to honour so should she, at his prayer,
accept a noble man whom he loves better than all men and whom
she will love too. This she does at last.

In the story, Rossetti portrays himself as a young king (an appropriate enough figure) who has gone hunting with his friend, a
young knight. Both men are thirsty and stop at a Forester's cottage where a young girl brings them a cup of water. Both men, of
course, fall in love with her 'unequalled beauty.'

The story then tells how the king is already engaged to a
princess, a woman 'worthy of all love' who probably represents
Lizzie Sidall. Morris in his guise as the young knight, and regardless of all social considerations, now goes to beg the Forester for
his daughter's hand. The girl however has fixed her heart on the
king whose rank she does not know. When she learns of it, she
resolves to die rather than wed another.

According to the story, Morris then went to Rossetti to beg his
help. A fairy tale ending follows. The king goes to the girl and
pleads his friend's cause while revealing his own love for her.
Rather than giving way to mutual passion however, honour and
friendship triumph. Just as the king sacrifices true love for duty,
so the Forester's daughter is begged to '. . . accept a noble man
whom he loves better than all men and whom she will love too'.
The Forester's daughter eventually agrees.

If this little story suggests the broad outlines of what happened
between Morris, Rossetti and Jane, the real course of events
seems to have been more complex. While Morris was making
another of his expeditions to France, Rossetti returned to
Oxford, ostensibly to work on the unfinished murals in the
Union. It was while on this visit that he drew Jane in the guise of
Queen Guenevere. The drawing itself is particularly intense and
is a powerful revelation of Jane's allure. The sombre, downcast
eyes are filled with a passion all the more forceful for its am-
biguity, while her luxuriant, dark and glossy hair radiates that

enslaving abundance through which the Pre-Raphaelite's women so often lured their lovers. Soon the drawing was in London and the object of much admiration among Rossetti's friends.

The strain on Morris himself was beginning to take its toll, however. He had vowed himself to art, but abandoned architecture in less than a year. Under the dominating influence of Rossetti he had taken up painting but laboured with little success. He had also fallen in love with a woman for whose affection, as Rossetti's story seems to suggest, he knew he had to compete. His poems, admired by a few men of discernment, many of whom he did not know, had been savagely received by the reviewers.

During the year that Jane was preparing for her marriage, Morris passed through a period of the deepest unhappiness. Mackail writes of this time with his characteristic discretion, saying of his hero: 'the instability which he found, or thought he found, in his own character, became for a time acute. The overstrain of the crowded years through which he had been passing with all their inward revolutions, their pangs of growth and fevers of imagination had left him, like some lover in his own poems, languid and subject to strange fluctuations of mood.' Morris was, it seems, on the edge of a nervous breakdown.

Nonetheless, on 26 April 1859 the wedding took place in Saint Michael's Church, Oxford. No member of the Morris family was present, nor was Rossetti there. The bride's father gave her away. Charles Faulkner was the best man. The newly ordained Richard Dixon, more nervous than the rest, stumbled over his words and joined 'William and Mary' in holy wedlock. The couple then left for a six week honeymoon which took them to Paris, Ghent, Bruges, Cologne and up the Rhine to Basle. On their return, and after a short period in London, Morris installed his bride in the Red House, the 'palace of art' he had commissioned for them in the Kent countryside. After a period of great stress, five years of radiant and dream-like happiness were about to open before him.

Opposite: *It was while decorating the Oxford Union that Morris and Rossetti both fell in love with Jane Burden. Rossetti's portrait suggests the exotic mystique of her beauty. The richness of Jane's hair, the fullness of her lips and her deep, slow eyes were to become an obsession.*

ARTISTS AND ENTREPRENEURS

It was while in France with Philip Webb that Morris first discussed plans for the Red House. His vision was of something 'very medieval in spirit,' and initial ideas were enthusiastically jotted down in Morris's railway timetable. Eventually, an orchard and meadow in the Kentish village of Upton, ten miles from London, were bought, and by April 1859 Webb had completed his drawings for what was to be one of the most influential collaborative exercises in the history of English design.

We have seen that for Morris, architecture was the foundation of all the arts, an essential and even definitively human activity. It embraced, he declared: 'the whole external surroundings of the life of man; we cannot escape from it if we would so long as we are part of civilisation, for it means the moulding and altering to human needs of the very face of the earth itself . . . it concerns us all, and needs the help of all.' The building of the Red House was thus the expression of some of Morris's most deeply held beliefs.

Nonetheless, the building should not be seen as heralding a revolution in English architecture. It was the followers of the later Arts and Crafts Movement, needing a suitable shrine for their patron saint, who elevated the Red House to this spuriously innovative status. The building is in fact a particularly fine example of the best secular design of the mid Nineteenth Century Gothic Revival, a natural development of the work of Street and William Butterfield, architects who, in their domestic buildings, had effected a bold simplification of Gothic detail. The free and functionally based planning of the Red House stems from this tradition, as do the picturesque, high hipped roofs of tile and the brick walls which give the building its name.

The Red House, developed out of an intensely argued concern with the nature of Gothic, is both romantic and solid. In conformity with Morris's ideals, it is an expression of life worthily lived and so at one with the sensitively shaped natural world that surrounds it. Indeed, Morris was so determined that the orchard in which his home was situated should complement the building itself that the Red House was planned in a way that necessitated hardly a tree being felled. On hot autumn days, guests were surprised as apples tumbled in at the open windows.

The garden too was part of this alliance of art and nature. Indeed, it was one of the loveliest features of the house and a clear development of that intense delight in flowers that had characterised Morris from his childhood. Georgina Burne-Jones, a frequent visitor, described how the garden at the front '... was spaced formally into four little square gardens making a big square together, each of the smaller squares had a wattled fence round it with an opening by which one entered, and all over the fences roses grew thickly'. Her description is irresistibly reminiscent of the gardens in the illuminated manuscripts of the Middle Ages where lovers plight their troth.

Out of this abundance of nature rose the two-storied, L-shaped building with its steep, irregular roofs and weathervane designed in thin, beautifully contrived counterpoint, and ornamented both with Morris's initials and the horse's head suggested by his family coat-of-arms. The walls are partly covered with a light tracery of ivy, while the varieties of window—sash, lancet and circular—are recessed. Where appropriate, they are surmounted with blind pointed arches of brick. The exterior doors are again surrounded by pointed brick arches, while the conical roof and timber construction of the well add to the medieval flavour. For Morris, the design of the whole exemplified what he most admired, 'the style of the thirteenth century'.

Though the interior of the Red House appeared to visitors as 'severely simple and grand', it is incorrect to see it as a wholesale reaction to the darkness and confused clutter normally associated with High Victorian design. Indeed, rather than marking a clean break with the age, the rooms and their furnishings show an interesting re-interpretation of many received ideas.

To wealthier Victorians especially, the home was a shrine that stood in sharp distinction to the uncomfortable, threatening world beyond its walls. It was at once embued with heightened feelings of honesty, integrity and love, while in its ostentatious display it could take on the qualities of both a palace of illusions and a 'joyful nook of heaven in an unheavenly world'. As the century progressed, so the home also became the special domain of the woman whose taste and virtue it was designed to represent. In the 1860s however—at the time Morris was building the Red House it was still generally the man who had the choice of domestic furnishings. In this, of course, Morris was no exception, and the values of beauty and integrity, of the Gothic revived and refashioned into a palace of art, were conventional notions to which he brought the particular stamp of his personality.

He had a dark if magnificent interior on which to work. The entrance hall establishes the tone of the house. It is tiled in rich red, while a fine oak staircase, its solidity offset by simple circular perforations and majestic pinnacled newel-posts, leads the eye up past blind brick arcades over the doors to a richly patterned roof supported by exposed beams. The walls are bare, but the original intention was to cover them with tempera paintings representing scenes from the tale of Troy.

Something of the richness of this proposed effect can be judged from Webb's massive settle-cupboard with its painted scenes from the medieval *Nibelungenlied*, variously attributed to Rossetti, Burne-Jones and Morris himself. Burne-Jones certainly designed some of the stained-glass in the windows down the side of the long gallery.

To harmonise with the exterior and the arches over the doors, fireplaces were built of rubbed red brick, the patterns created by their bonding offsetting their monumental design. Some are further inscribed with mottoes: 'Our content is our best having' and '*Ars Longa Vita Brevis*'. This was a motif later to be repeated on the copper repousse panels of many pieces of Arts and Crafts furniture.

The furniture in the Red House itself is similarly impressive. A great Gothic dresser stood in the dining room, while along with a wardrobe painted by Burne-Jones with scenes from Chaucer's *The Prioress's Tale*, the great settle was moved in from Red Lion Square and placed at the end of the drawing room. Webb now superimposed a minstrels' gallery on it. It was Webb who designed the greater part of the furniture for Red House: oak tables, beds and chairs, grates, fire irons and brass candlesticks.

Others contributed to the frescoes and tapestry work. Morris had boasted he would make the drawing room the most beautiful in England. This area occupies the external L of the building and is lit by a window that originally looked over the Kent countryside. A smaller, west-facing oriel window was designed to catch the evening sun as it fell on the tapestries and painted walls. This scheme too was never completed, but while Morris and Jane covered the ceiling with a floral pattern, Rossetti painted 'The Salutation of Beatrice' on the doors of the settle and Burne-Jones began to decorate the walls with scenes from the medieval romance of *Sire Degrevaunt*.

Embroidery was also to be an important part of the design scheme, and here Jane showed her undoubted ability. No suitable decorated fabrics could be found on the market, though Jane discovered a length of indigo-dyed blue serge on which Morris created a design of simple, stylised plants derived from a manuscript in the British Museum. This Jane then worked in a couched running stitch. 'The work went quickly,' she wrote, 'and when we finished we covered the walls of the bedroom at Red House to our great joy.' These hangings may have been among those later displayed in the Medieval Court of the 1862 International Exhibition and which won an award. They now hang at Kelmscott Manor.

Morris himself had started experiments in embroidery before he met Jane, working with his own hands a hanging with a bird and tree motif. This was further embroidered with his personal motto 'If I Can'. The influence of Street is clear. With his concern for quality in all the handicrafts, Street had recommended a return to the study of medieval English embroidery and the glories of *opus anglicum*. He had written: 'Undertake works which exhibit the industry, the intellect and the good taste of the worker.' While Morris's early design is far from successful—the stylised birds in particular are very weak compared to his mature work—he was throughout his life to encourage the women of his acquaintance to take up embroidery, and later results were excellent.

After he met Jane, for example, Morris helped her develop her skills as a needlewoman. 'We studied old pieces by unpicking,' she wrote. 'We learnt very much but it was uphill work and only carried through by his enormous energy and perseverance.' Jane's own energy and perseverance were far from inconsiderable however, and one large but uncompleted scheme on which she worked was an embroidered and appliquéd hanging of the twelve *Illustrious Women*, its subjects vaguely drawn from Boccaccio, Chaucer and Tennyson. The figures were designed to be worked on plain linen, cut out and appliquéd to sumptuous backgrounds of heavy silk. Three of these panels can now be seen in the Green Drawing Room in the Victoria and Albert Museum.

Right: *Jane Morris became a highly accomplished needlewoman and these embroidered panels suggest how her skills were united with those of Morris and his friends to create the beautiful artefacts for Red House which were later to give a stimulus to the founding of the Firm.*

Taken as a whole, these decorative schemes for the Red House suggest a group of highly talented young people dissatisfied with the poor quality of nearly all the commercial manufacture then available and creating by their own energies an environment in which objects embued with their medieval dreams created a small but exquisite palace of art.

Left: *The upper landing at Red House showing stained glass and one of the Gothic newel posts.*

The atmosphere was not however one of vague daydreaming. There were genuine discoveries, innovation and hard work. There were also riotous high spirits. Couples such as the Burne-Joneses, the Rossettis and the Maddox-Browns, along with such single young men as Charles Faulkner, Arthur Hughes and Swinburne were met at the station each weekend in a bright wagonette designed for Morris by Webb. Jane and Georgina Burne-Jones in particular derived much pleasure from driving round the Kent countryside in this after a morning spent over their needlework. In the evening they would return to regale the men with stories of what they had seen.

It is recounted how, towards supper-time, Morris himself would descend to his cellar and reappear, beaming with joy, his hands grasped round bottles of wine while other bottles were tucked under his arms. Later, there were games of hide-and-seek or songs round the piano. Occasionally, things got a little wilder and Morris himself—forbearing despite his temper—became the butt of practical jokes. On one occasion, for example, it was discovered that Charles Faulkner had stored a supply of windfall apples in the gallery over the settle. With these he defended himself against all comers until one too expertly aimed missile gave Morris a black eye. Sometimes on the mornings following, Morris—who was still concerned about his broadening figure—would get up and find his waistcoat did not fit. His guests had sewn tucks in it during the night. 'You fellows have been at it again,' he would declare with good humour.

There were problems gathering to cloud that good-humour, however. Morris's income from the shares in the Devon mine was beginning to diminish. Further, in January 1861 his oldest daughter Jenny was born, followed by his second, May, the next year. Morris was acquiring responsibilities. Though financial anxiety was not yet acute, it helped to focus his mind.

He had by now considerable experience of organising, inspiring and participating in the many skills required in decorating a home. He had a superlative eye for quality, an unrivalled sense of the design potential of texture, colour and pattern. He also had friends who had proved the range of their talents from architecture, through furniture making, stained glass and metalwork to embroidery. What they had made they had produced in response to the poor quality of the manufactures generally available. Might there not be a wider market for this? 'The idea came to him,' Burne-Jones wrote, 'of beginning a manufactury of all things necessary for the decoration of a house.'

For a long time the whole scheme was somewhat casual, as perhaps it needed to be. An unsecured loan of £100 from Morris's family and shares of £1 a head served to give the arrangement the appearance of a definite basis, but the spirit of enlightened amateurism remained. Theodore Watts-Dunton, the solicitor who had saved Swinburne from self-destructive bohemianism, recalled Rossetti as saying: 'In fact, it was a mere playing at business, and Morris was elected manager, not because we ever dreamed he would turn out a man of business, but because he was the only one of us who had the time and money to spare. We had no idea whatever of commercial success, but it succeeded almost in our own despite.'

Whether it was 'playing at business' or not, a prospectus was clearly needed to advertise the intentions of Morris, Marshall, Faulkner and Co. whose partners now described themselves as 'Fine Art Workmen in Painting, Carving, Furniture, and the Metals'. Faulkner was to receive £150 a year as their bookkeeper. Morris was to receive a similar salary for his work as manager.

Peter Paul Marshall, a surveyor and occasional designer, remains
a vague figure of little apparent importance to the Firm.

The growth of Decorative Art in this country, owing to the efforts
of English Architects, has now reached a point at which it seems
desirable that Artists of reputation should devote their time to it.
Although no doubt particular instances of success may be cited,
still it must be generally felt that attempts of this kind hitherto
have been crude and fragmentary. Up to this time, the want of
that artistic supervision, which can alone bring about harmony
between the various parts of a successful work, has been
increased by the necessarily excessive outlay, consequent on
taking one individual artist from his pictorial labours.

The Artists whose names appear above hope by association to
do away with this difficulty. Having among their number men of
varied qualifications, they will be able to undertake any species
of decoration, mural or otherwise, from pictures, properly so-
called, down to the consideration of the smallest work susceptible
of art beauty. It is anticipated that by such co-operation, the
largest amount of what is essentially the artist's work, along with
his constant supervision, will be secured at the smallest possible
expense, while the work done must necessarily be of a much more
complete order, than if any single artist were incidentally
employed in the usual manner.

These artists having for many years been deeply attached to
the study of the Decorative Arts of all times and countries, have
felt more than most people the want of some one place, where
they could either obtain or get produced work of a genuine and
beautiful character. They have therefore now established
themselves as a firm, for the production, by themselves and
under their supervision of—

I. Mural Decoration, either in Pictures or in Pattern Work, or
merely in the arrangement of Colours, as applied to dwelling-
houses, churches, or public buildings.
II. Carving generally, as applied to Architecture.
III. Stained Glass, especially with reference to its harmony
with Mural Decoration.
IV. Metal Work in all its branches, including Jewellery.
V. Furniture, either depending for its beauty on its own
design, on the application of materials hitherto overlooked, or
on its conjunction with Figure and Pattern Painting. Under
this head is included Embroidery of all kinds, Stamped
Leather, and ornamental work in other such materials, besides
every article necessary for domestic use.

It is only necessary to state further, that work of all the above
classes will be estimated for, and executed in a business-like

*The Prospectus of Morris,
Marshall, Faulkner and Co
clearly defines their aims.*

manner; and it is believed that good decoration, involving rather the luxury of taste than the luxury of costliness, will be found to be much less expensive than is generally supposed.

The opening paragraphs of the prospectus are interesting for a number of reasons. They suggest, first of all, a fairly widespread discontent at the state of the applied arts in England and locate the origins of this in a lack of artistic 'supervision' over manufacture. With the propagandist simplicity characteristic of such literature, the prospectus also claims that where 'Artists of reputation' have been involved in production, their attempts have been 'crude and fragmentary'. The reason put forward is the expense involved in luring an artist away from his more profitable pictorial labours.

The great change advocated by the partners of the Firm was the idea of 'association', the belief that a group of artists working on a cooperative and profit-sharing basis, would be able to afford to devote their time and skills fully to design and supervision. In other words, they would be able to make their living (or an adequate part of their living) from this sort of work, while also lowering the cost of goods to the customer.

This close involvement of the artist in manufacture had its roots deep in the thought of Ruskin and other critics of industrialisation. It does not mean, however, that the Firm was advocating a return to wholesale craftsman manufacture—the idea that the designer and the maker should invariably be one man. The key word here is 'supervision'. So far, the prospectus claims, this had proved prohibitively expensive and so there had not commonly been a 'harmony between the various parts of a successful work.' It is precisely this measure of 'supervision' that Morris, Marshall, Faulkner and Co would be able to provide. In other words, although manufacture would still be based on the division of labour, on various individuals bringing different single skills to the many processes of production, these individuals would no longer be disparate, disinterested and alienated from their labour. They would be brought closer to the designer would the designer would be brought closer to them.

There is no question here of a revolution in the means of production. Rather, production would be significantly modified. It would be brought under the watchful eye of a true artist and designer instead of being placed under the regular inspection of a capitalist and his accountants. The division of labour has not been abandoned. It has been centred on the influence of a true craftsman who would ensure that the results of his workers' labour were an organic whole. For the most part, of course, that craftsman was Morris himself.

The range of products and services offered in the prospectus reflects the skills of those working on the Red House: mural painting, architectural ornament (though not architecture itself), stained glass, metal work, furniture making and embroidery. These are the areas where, the prospectus claims, manufacture has been on the whole been of a low quality.

Left: *The artist craftsmen of the Firm were not the only people involved in trying to establish a style superior to that of conventional Victorian taste. William Burges, for example, was experimenting with painted furniture and producing highly sophisticated pieces such as this bookcase. Here the colour is an essential feature in the construction, revealing its architecture rather than being merely applied to the surface.*

In the broadest terms, this may well be correct. The works exhibited in the Medieval Court of the International Exhibition of 1862 however—the event which brought the Firm to real prominence—strongly suggest that Morris, Marshall, Faulkner and Co were not spearheading a revolution in design but contributing to the styles of the avant-garde. It is therefore important to see their work in context. The International Exhibition of 1862 is a useful vantage point from which to do this since, in the Medieval Court itself, there was gathered together the work of the leading living representatives of the Gothic revival: Burges, Bodley, Butterfield, Scott and Street, as well as Webb, Morris and other members of the Firm.

As with architecture so in the applied arts, one of the great influences revealed here is Pugin, perhaps the finest of all the architects and designers of the Gothic Revival. Like the partners in the Firm, Pugin had worked in a variety of fields of applied art: metalwork, wood and stone carving, tiles, furniture and wallpaper. His revolt against machine production was based on a contempt for its results and was fuelled by his profound religious convictions and advanced ideas on function and ornament.

For Pugin, style and faith were one, and the only true expressions of both were medieval, Roman Catholic and Gothic. Any other style was pagan and therefore morally and aesthetically repugnant. Furthermore, in Pugin's view, beauty derives from function. 'Glaring, showy, and meretricious ornament,'—the dominant style of the Great Exhibition, in fact—reveals 'the false notion of disguising instead of beautifying articles of utility.' Ornament, Pugin declared, should be no more than 'enrichment of the essential composition'. This can be seen in his furniture. In combination with J. G. Crace, Pugin made some of the most magnificent furniture of the nineteenth century: carved, enriched with crisp tracery yet clear in its constructional elements: strong legs, stretchers, braces and so on.

Both Street and Butterfield developed this work towards a more solid style, especially in their church architecture, and Webb sketched the work of both. Something of the ideals behind such pieces are given in Bruce Talbert's *Gothic Forms Applied to Furniture* where he suggests that in medieval work '. . . the wood is solid, the construction honestly shown, and fastened by tenons, pegs, iron clasps, etc'. These are very clearly the virtues of the table designed by Webb in c. 1860 with its scrubbed oak top, boarded sides and stout, chamfered legs terminating in castellated bases.

Though Morris himself designed no furniture for the Firm, the painted pieces they exhibited in the 1862 Exhibition clearly derive from the experiments he and Rossetti had made with Burne-Jones during the early years in Red Lion Square. This is what Morris himself called 'state furniture'.

These pieces were almost certainly influenced by William Burges whose designs for painted furniture in the proposed cathedral at Lille Morris had seen while a student with Street. Burges's *Yatman Cabinet* and magnificent bookcase of 1859–62 develop this mode and show an understanding of the principles and possibilities of painted furniture far more sophisticated than the Firm's.

Burges's painted pieces were, first of all, designed as an integral part of his sumptuous Gothic interiors such as Lord Bute's Cardiff Castle which is one of the wonders of the period. In addition, they reveal a scholarly understanding of medieval practices and their imaginative recreation. Where the pieces made by the Firm are essentially furniture that has been painted, Burges's painting is part of the design as a whole, while the subjects of the figure panels especially are closely identified with the general purpose of the item. Thus the magnificent bookcase designed to hold Burges's collection of art books is covered with scenes representing incidents in the history of art from both the pagan and Christian periods.

Burges's bookcase is also interesting as a highly sophisticated exercise in artistic collaboration and suggests a level of co-operation and supervision the Firm could not yet achieve. The bookcase is a display of Burges's own architectonic powers, while the list of painters who worked on it makes up a roll-call of Pre-Raphaelite talent great and small. These painters include Rossetti, Burne-Jones and the Simeon Solomon, among others.

Compared to this, the pieces by the Firm are simplistic. Indeed, the cabinet painted by Burne-Jones with *The Back-gammon Players* is distinctly crude when compared to Burges's work, though the *Saint George Cabinet*, now in the Victoria and Albert Museum, is a somewhat superior piece. Webb's architectonic skill can be seen in the design of the legs especially, while the panels by Morris show what he could sometimes achieve in figure drawing. The panel on the far left in which the king turns huddled in his grief while the princess is led away by armoured soldiers with cruel diagonal pikes is particularly effective.

Below: *The* Saint George Cabinet *of 1862 is one of the Firm's best-known pieces of painted furniture and has panels by Morris himself. These are dramatically drawn and well executed and should be compared to those on Burges's bookcase in the preceding illustration.*

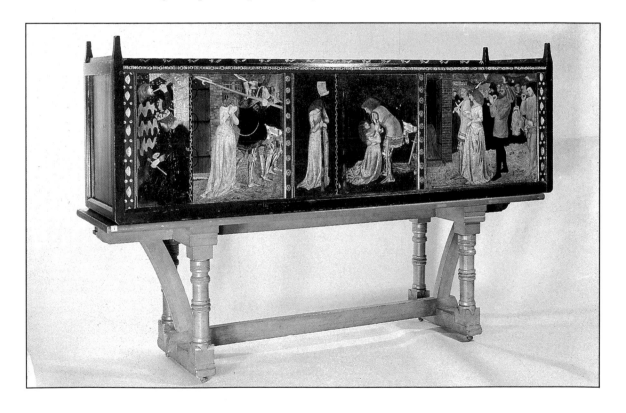

The Firm also showed in the Exhibition of 1862 tiles painted by Rossetti, Burne-Jones, Webb and Morris. Though after 1866 tile production which incorporated figures in the design largely disappeared from the Firm's output (ceramic work was often sub-contracted to William de Morgan) their manufacture shows the Firm's methods in a number of interesting lights.

For example, the basic tiles were bought in rather than made by the Firm itself, but were painted and fired on the premises. This was both a laborious and a skilful process. A cartoon was first drawn. Often, as in the case of Burne-Jones's fairy tale cycles, these had a certain quiet humour and charm. Rather than being printed onto the tiles however, the outlines of the design were copied by hand and then filled in and fired. Faulkner, his sister and Georgina Burne-Jones were chiefly employed here. While such labour undoubtedly contributed to the hand-finished look Morris required, it also resulted in the tiles themselves being five times the cost of those normally manufactured. Furthermore, their fragile nature meant that they could not be used to cover floors but were to be mounted over fireplaces or in decorative panels such as that designed for the house of the watercolourist Birkett Foster.

Morris's first collection of wallpapers also dates from this period. These again show his work in an interesting perspective, for each of these early designs—*Trellis*, *Daisy* and *Fruit*—is markedly old-fashioned for its time. This stems in part from Morris's inexperience with the formal problems of wallpaper design and his greater familiarity with tile and embroidery work. It is also to some degree a reaction to advanced tastes, and an early if relatively naive expression of some of those characteristics which were later to make Morris the greatest pattern designer of his age. Once again, it is important to know the context if Morris's work is to be seen in its proper perspective.

Right: *Morris's original design for* Trellis *with birds by Phillip Webb.*

Opposite: *The subtle use of motifs in Morris's early wallpaper* Fruit *(1864) was much influenced by the tile design he was also interested in at this time.*

Repellently gaudy attempts at the three-dimensional and illustrative such as Heywood, Higginbottom and Smith's *Crystal Palace* wallpaper of 1851, had prompted a number of designers to rethink the principles on which they worked. The leading figures here were two: Pugin, whose sumptuous wallpapers for the Houses of Parliament with their strong interlacing of foliage and heraldic motifs are triumphs of colour and the repeated, two dimensional motif; and that eclectic master of abstract and geometric form Owen Jones.

Jones was part of a circle which included a number of the more advanced thinkers on design, men who had been influenced by Pugin but were not wholly subdued to his principles. They included William Dyce, the architect Matthew Digby Wyatt and Henry Cole who, under the pseudonym Felix Summerly, had designed a prize-winning tea set for Minton's and founded Summerly's Fine Art Manufacturers, a precursor of Morris's Firm. Their *Journal of Design and Manufactures* had also attempted to propagate 'sound principles of ornamental art' and to criticise items that failed to meet their standards. Indeed, the editors went so far as including in their magazine actual samples of textiles and wallpapers of which they approved.

Many of these last have a delightful freshness and freedom, while those by Dyce and Owen Jones especially conform to 'the proper impression of flatness'. Jones indeed had an exceptional knowledge of two dimensional design—his *Grammar of Ornament* became a basic source book—and his principles can be seen in his black, white and purple chintz of 1851. His watercolour designs for wallpaper also show how he could use plant forms in a way that juxtaposes the naturalistic and the abstract in a satisfying equilibrium.

Morris however, whose response to plant-forms was deeper and more sensuous than Jones's, '. . . disliked *flowers* treated geometrically stiffly in patterns'. His three earliest wallpaper designs show this clearly. In *Daisy*, for example, the powdering of the lightly formalised motifs over the stippled background means that there is no complexity in the linking and masking of repeats. In *Trellis*, the wooden structure that gives the paper its name also supplies the sense of regular two-dimensional pattern while providing a foil for the meandering and realistic design of flowers, leaves and birds. A simplified version of this idea was used again in what is perhaps Morris's first printed cotton, the *Jasmine Trail* of 1868–70.

In *Fruit*, Morris's attempt to give a regular scheme to lightly stylised naturalistic motifs derived in part from tile manufacture. Each repeat is here subdivided into four squares filled by a diagonal design. The effect is a satisfying one since the eye is beguiled by the counterpoint between each of the four squares and the

Left: *Two exteriors of Red House, Morris's 'palace of art' in the Kent countryside.*

larger repeats which these make up.

All of these early papers are naturalistic in a way that harks back to principles of design realism popular twenty years earlier, yet each is also clearly embued with Morris's own sense of weight and balance. The papers did not prove a great commercial success however, and no more designs were produced until the early 1870s when Morris's genius for such work was to flourish with a sudden abundance.

It was stained glass manufacture that proved to be the greatest achievement of these early years of the Firm. Indeed, it was in this field that Morris, Marshall, Faulkner and Co made their most outstanding contribution to the art of the nineteenth century Gothic revival. All of Morris's skills were called on here: his ability to harness the talents of others and work in cooperation with them, his readiness to join the problems of design to the details of manufacture, his daring technical experiment and, finally, that scholarly love of the Middle Ages which showed him how the

Right: *The St Paul window at All Saints' Church, Selsley, Gloucestershire shows the clear influence of Phillip Webb on the Firm's early work. Later stained glass windows were to develop a more dramatic and sumptuous approach.*

craftsmen of the past had triumphed by developing the natural qualities of the medium in which they worked. The best of the Firm's windows have a brilliance of colour, an understanding of pictorial composition and a fertility of invention that are truly remarkable. In a few years, Morris and his colleagues raised an ancient technique to heights that had not been reached for three hundred years.

By reading the enclosed you will see that I have started as a decorator which I have long meant to do when I could get men of reputation to join me, and to this end mainly I have built my fine house. You see we are, or consider ourselves to be, the only really artistic firm of the kind, the others being only glass painters in point of fact, (like Clayton & Bell) or else that curious nondescript mixture of clerical tailor and decorator that flourishes in Southampton Street, Strand; whereas we shall do—most things. However, what we are most anxious to get at present is wall-decoration, and I want to know if you could be so kind as to send me (without troubling yourself) a list of clergymen and others, to whom it *might* be any use to send a circular. In about a month we shall have some things to show in these rooms, painted cabinets, embroidery and all the rest of it, and perhaps you could look us up then: I suppose till the holidays you couldn't come down to Red House: I was very much disappointed that you called when I was out before.

Morris wrote this letter to his old tutor Rev. Guy asking for help in finding commissions for the Firm.

They were helped by a comparatively recent upsurge of interest in medieval stained glass design and manufacture. In reaction to eighteenth century ideas about the medium—the belief that stained glass should closely approximate the effects of classical easel painting—a number of enthusiasts had returned to examining older traditions. Francis Wilson Oliphant, for example, in his *Plea for Stained Glass*, had urged consideration of the natural qualities of the medium over a painterly approach, but the most influential figure here was Charles Winston. In his *Inquiry into the Differences of Style observable in Ancient Glass Paintings, especially in England: with Hints on Glass Painting*, Winston urged '... preserving the brilliancy and general transparency of glass, and of promoting the distinctiveness of the design by the use of clear lights, transparent shadows, and strong contrasts of light and shade'. He urged the 'mosaic system' of glass painting in which 'each colour of the design, except yellow, brown, and black, must be represented by a separate pane of glass'. In addition, Winston offered a translation of an important medieval treatise on glass as well as an excellent and influential series of illustrative plates.

Others were working on the technical problems of producing a glass that was close to medieval textures while having colours that more nearly approximated medieval tints. Pugin and John Hardman, for example, had reintroduced the use of 'pot metal' or 'flashed' glass which, flattened from the glassblower's original bubble, is beautifully thick, uneven and streaky. Pugin also worked on stylised and symbolic designs for windows, while Winston commissioned experiments in the chemistry of colour analysis which eventually led to Powell and Sons of Whitefriars producing colours of a medieval luminosity. Workers such as George Campfield, who became Morris's studio foreman, were trained in the newly revived techniques, and it was on this basis that the Firm itself could build.

To avoid the mere mechanical repetition of old styles they needed designers of exceptional talent. Here the combined skills of several partners in the Firm produced a remarkable homogeneity of effect. Rossetti was responsible for some thirty designs, including the best domestic glass. Ford Maddox Brown produced three times this number, while a further one hundred and fifty designs were contributed by Morris himself. It was Burne-Jones however who was to become the designer of central importance. In the Exhibition of 1862 he had shown a distinctly Pre-Raphaelite *Annunciation*, a composition which skilfully exploited the two-dimensional possibilities of stained glass design. He had also worked on some advanced if fussy windows for Oxford Cathedral and Waltham Abbey. In the over-all design of the early large stained glass schemes of the Firm however Morris and Webb were the key figures. Morris was responsible for the colour, while layout was chiefly in the hands of Webb.

Many of the Firm's early ecclesiastical commissions came from the Gothic architect G.F. Bodley, and the windows they made for Bodley's All Saints', Selsley, Gloucestershire show Webb's influence clearly. The fenestration in All Saints' is irregular, but is given a sense of unity by Webb's decision to create a band of richly coloured panels running at a uniform height. Each panel has similar borders and is set in 'quarries' or backgrounds of identical pale glass. The effect is light and comparatively simple compared to the Firm's mature work, and the success of this basic scheme was copied in a number of other early commissions, including St Michael's, Brighton. Here the east window in the South Aisle is by Morris and represents *The Three Maries at the Sepulchre*.

This pair of windows shows Morris's early design at its best. The difficulties he had with drawing and draping the human figure—difficulties evident in his work at Selsley—are here less evident if not completely resolved. There is still a little ungainliness in the way the Angel of the Resurrection is sitting on the empty tomb, but the space between this figure and the Maries themselves is most dramatically conceived. The use of colour is also excellent. The whites and pale golds are beautifully and subtley various and serve as an excellent foil to the deep greens of the ground, the rich rubies of the Angel's wings and the blue of the Virgin's robe which seems to give this figure a nobility and quiet prominence that are truly dramatic.

It is clear that in addition to concerning himself with the colour schemes and compositional details of the windows, Morris was also increasingly interested in the design problems that arose when trying to bring a unity of effect to large windows in particular. The East window of St Michael's, Lyndhurst, for example, is a *tour de force* of decorative design. The stone tracery here is especially complex, but by subdividing the lancets and placing within each panel groups of figures who turn towards the Virgin—the central and only full-faced figure in the window—Morris achieved a remarkably dynamic and uniform impression of worship in the New Jerusalem.

The East window at Middleton Cheney is again both a remarkable piece of design and cooperation, for no less than five artists worked on this piece. Morris himself was responsible for the simple but excellent panel of Eve and the Virgin, while the dramatic banners of the Tribes of Israel, which so excitingly break into the borders of the upper panels, are the work of Webb. Burne-Jones, Maddox Brown and Simeon Solomon contributed other panels.

It is with the windows at St Mary's, Bloxham, however that Morris reached the heights of his early achievement. By this time Webb's contribution had been reduced to such details as providing designs for the architectural background of the walls of the Holy City while Morris was responsible for the over-all arrangement. The advance from the early windows at Selsley is marked. The quarries have been abandoned, and the resulting effect is darker and richer. The grounds of the individual panels are ornamented with the designs Morris had developed for this purpose. Above all, the figures have an importance and expressiveness that goes far beyond the earlier work. The dominance of architectural principles of composition has been replaced by more assuredly pictorial concerns. The way had thus been prepared for the great windows of the late 1860s and early '70s which Morris was to produce in collaboration with Burne-Jones.

The first London centre for many of these activities was 8 Red Lion Square, a few doors away from where Morris and Burne-Jones had once lodged. The Firm rented the first floor as their office and showroom and part of the basement for the workshop. Here they built their kiln for firing glass and tiles.

Opposite: *The East Window of All Saints', Middleton Cheney, Northamptonshire, dates from 1865 and is a triumphant example of the Firm's work in this medium. The sense of procession gives the window a sense of drama, while the contrast between the saints, the angels, and the top panel representing the worship of the mystic Lamb, lifts the observer from the human to the heavenly through a subtle use of colour.*

Right: *Morris himself was responsible for* Eve and the Virgin *in the Middleton Cheney window. The figures represent the fall and the promise of salvation, and reveal Morris's strengths and limitations as a draughtsman. While the two women are well differentiated, they are drawn in profile rather than the more complex postures adopted by many of the figures elsewhere in this part of the window.*

What had started as an amateur venture only slowly became more professional. Here the force of Morris's personality and his immense energy were of the utmost importance. So too was the courage of his commitment. In addition to being involved in every aspect of the Firm's design and manufacture (often with somewhat deleterious effects on its efficiency) he increased its share capital, secured more loans and advanced all of his own money that he could afford. This was perhaps the only time in his life that he had pressing financial problems. Occasionally, the Firm actually showed a loss, and there were times when Morris's colleagues were worried as his anxiety and over-work became evident.

The amateurism and high spirits continued for some time, however. Weekly meetings of the Firm, beginning at eight or

nine in the evening, would open with the retelling of anecdotes, develop into arguments about medieval art, and only turn to matters of business some three hours later. Practical jokes, many of them directed against Morris himself, still helped to diffuse too serious an air.

Towards his customers Morris adopted a blunt and even dictatorial air. He gave the impression that he did not care very much whether he received their orders or not. Nor did he greatly mind how he looked. The public were confronted by a burly man, very obviously a gentleman, dressed in a blue worker's shirt and a round hat. His hands were quite likely to be dirty from his labours. The prices of the goods were high and the prices were as marked. There was no haggling and no willingness to make slight alterations to suit a buyer's whim. A bluff, take it or leave it air characterised buying items from Morris, Marshall, Faulkner and Co. The public, of course, was hugely intrigued.

But regular journeys up and down to the Red House greatly added to the nervous strain. When Morris eventually caught a chill which turned into rheumatic fever he had to face a painful decision. Burne-Jones could not be prevailed on to move to Kent and into a proposed extension of the Red House. There was therefore no alternative but to sell the place. The Burne-Joneses paid their last visit in September 1865. Two months later, Morris himself had gone. The wrench was exceedingly painful for him and he never returned. The days in the palace of art were over, and before the busy, harassed idealist there now stretched an unsuspected wilderness of inner desolation and pain.

Morris's letter to Burne-Jones about giving up Red House shows both the depth of his feelings and his immense animal vitality.

As to our palace of Art, I confess your letter was a blow to me at first, though hardly an unexpected one—in short I cried; but I have got over it now. As to our being a miserable lot, old chap, speaking for myself I don't know, I refuse to make myself really unhappy for any thing short of the loss of friends one can't do without. Suppose in all these troubles you had given us the slip what the devil should I have done? I am sure I couldn't have had the heart to have gone on with the firm: all our jolly subjects would have gone to pot—it frightens me to think of, Ned. But now I am only 30 years old, I shan't always have the rheumatism, and we shall have a lot of jolly years of invention and lustre plates together I hope. I need hardly tell you how I suffered for you in the worst of your troubles; on the Saturday I had begun a letter to you but it read so dismal (as indeed I felt little hope) that I burnt it. . . .

Left: *This photograph shows Morris in his working clothes. He could frequently be seen thus in the Firm's shop, and customers were often intrigued.*

'WHY SHOULD I STRIVE TO SET THE CROOKED STRAIGHT?'

In the autumn of 1865, the Firm moved its premises to 26 Queen Square, a spacious building in a somewhat rundown quarter of Bloomsbury. The ground floor was converted into an office and showroom, while the long corridor that led to what was once the ballroom housed the glasspainters. The ballroom itself became the principal workshop. Other workshops were crowded into the back of the house, while Morris and his family moved into the first floor. Far from residing in a palace of art, they were now living over the shop.

With the move came a new business manager, the hatchet-faced Warrington Taylor, 'ghastly thin but full of mental energy'. Taylor was a curiosity, yet the very range of his talents was invaluable to the Firm. The son of a Roman Catholic squire, educated at Eton with Swinburne and then in Germany, he had lost his money, joined the army and ended up as the cloakroom attendant at Her Majesty's Theatre, where he could indulge his taste for opera despite his limited means. Nonetheless, if Taylor had little control over his own financial affairs, he soon proved himself equal to sorting out those of Morris, Marshall, Faulkner and Co. 'Within a few months of his appointment,' recalled Georgina Burne-Jones, 'the rumour spread that he was keeping the accounts of the firm like a dragon, attending to the orders of customers, and actually getting Morris to work at one thing at a time.'

Taylor was a strange combination of the martinet and the Bohemian, and he clearly believed passionately in the work the Firm was doing. He also got rapidly to the root of its financial difficulties. Their annual expenditure was upwards of £1500 out of a turnover of £2000. Work was regularly undercharged and inefficiently managed. Salaries were high and Morris was wholly unrealistic about money at this stage. Private wealth had given him little sense of the logic of the account book and the need for self-discipline. 'I know the tendency at Queen Square to make life comfortable,' Taylor wrote in exasperation, 'anything rather than face death or a fact: hence the prosperous appearance of

Opposite: *Rossetti's portrait of Jane Morris as* Astarte Syriaca *is the most magnificent of all his many images of her. Here, as the ancient goddess of love, Jane seems to bear down on the viewer with all the power of the desire by which she has been imagined.*

Above: *This chair was produced by the Firm from c. 1865 onwards. It was based on a traditional Sussex design, comparatively cheap, and made for general sale.*

everything. Morris won't have many of the sours of life—can't get him to face that at all.' It is a telling comment.

Taylor was also aware that Morris was in the habit of drawing small cheques on petty cash and then being surprised at how these mounted up. Most of this money, it seems, went on books and wine. Taylor ordered Morris to cut the latter down to two and a half bottles a day. He then rallied the other partners, begging them to inspect the accounts weekly. 'See it done. . . See to it,' is a constant refrain in his letters.

Yet there was a strong anti-establishment streak in Taylor too. When the Firm won a commission to decorate the Armoury and Tapestry Rooms at St James's Palace, Taylor wrote to Webb, 'Remember we are embezzling public money now—what business has any palace to be decorated at all?' This nagging was to a purpose, however. Morris eventually accepted the need for greater regulation, and when Taylor died in 1870, the Firm was on a much sounder financial basis than it had been.

The commission for St James's Palace mentioned by Taylor was one of the most prestigious gained by the Firm in its early days and suggests how rapidly the partners' interior decorating skills came to be appreciated. Important examples of their work can be seen in both London and Cambridge.

Two decorating schemes for buildings in Cambridge both show the importance Morris attached to authenticity. In 1865–66, Morris had commissioned George Wardle to study the painted screens and roofs of the medieval churches in Norfolk and Suffolk, and to prepare drawings of these. Wardle did this with great enthusiasm, paying particular attention to colour combinations and the stencilling techniques the medieval decorators had used.

When they came to paint the roof of the nave of Jesus College chapel, the Firm was thus working on the basis of historical precedent. The result is a sumptuous checkerboard of armorial bearings and the Holy Initials supported by lines of painted angels. The scrolls held by these angels are a particularly effective device, providing as they do a lightly undulating white band, which both relieves the colour and emphasises the longitudinal and transverse directions of the roof itself.

For the dining hall of Queens, the Firm created an even brighter extravagance of high Victorian colour. Once again, however, the stencilled monograms, leaves and flowers are close to Wardle's drawings, as is the daring use of red and green, black and white and gold. To commission such a scheme was an act of great courage, and the completed work marks the Firm's last important work in the style of historical recreation.

The two London commissions were also for public rooms. Both were principally the work of Webb, and in both the layout

Left: *This cartoon of an angel holding a scroll dates from c. 1864 and was produced as part of the work for the decoration of the roof of the nave in Jesus College Chapel, Cambridge.*

of the decoration was fairly conventional. Where the Palace rooms have been somewhat altered however, the Green Dining Room in the Victoria and Albert Museum survives in its original state. It is thus an invaluable example of the Firm's decorating principles at this time.

The most immediately striking quality of the Green Dining Room is a sombre darkness relieved by glowing panels, gilded and ornamented with floral designs and figures. Above these, the walls have been painted green and patterned in relief, while a frieze of red and gold, decorated with hounds, is offset by the lighter pattern on the ceiling. The quality of the stained glass, placed in bands across a generous pale quarry, is high, and contributes again to the rich and even gloomy effect of the whole. Later Morris rooms were to be lighter, but the Green Dining Room remains as the most eloquent statement of the Firm's early ideas on the decoration of interiors and their desire to create a medieval sumptuousness.

Right: *The Green Dining Room in the Victoria and Albert Museum is one of the most famous of the Firm's early interiors. Though perhaps somewhat dark for modern tastes, its richly glowing colours and stained glass windows suggest the sumptuous effects aimed for in the Firm's earlier interior decoration work.*

This was the style that had also been aimed at in the Red House. Though the murals for that building were never completed, a suggestion of their possible effect can be gathered from some fragments of a verse tale of Troy which Morris wrote at this time.

Opposite: *The Hall of Queen's College, Cambridge.*

*This passage from Morris's
unfinished* Scenes from the Fall
of Troy *is a precursor of the
great period of narrative verse
writing he was now about to
enter.*

. . . Shall I say, Paris, that my heart is faint,
  And my head sick? I grow afraid of death:
  The gods are all against us, and some day
  The long black ships rowed equal on each side
  Shall throng the Trojan bay, and I shall walk
  From off the green earth to the straining ship;
  Cold Agamemnon with his sickly smile
  Shall go before me, and behind shall go
  My old chain Menelaus: we shall sit
  Under the deck amid the oars, and hear
  From day to day to their wretched measured beat
  Against the washing surges; they shall sit
  There in that twilight, with their faces turned
  Away from mine, and we shall say no word;
  And I shall be too sick at heart to sing,
  Though the dirt-grimed mariners may sing
  Through all their weariness their rowing-song
  Of Argo and the Golden Fleece, and Her
  That made and marred them all in a short while,
  As any potter might do with his clay,
  Medea the Colchian. . .

Here are men and women posed together or alone and reflecting sadly on both the lost innocence of love and the bloodthirstiness of chivalry. They stand like Pre-Raphaelite figures amid scenes vividly realised in their colour and detail. We are shown, for example, carp rising among the lilies and 'the few white tents and green log huts' of the Greek encampment. Though something of the brutality of the early work can still be felt, Morris's poetry was now moving away from the violence and ardour revealed in *The Defence of Guenevere* towards an altogether sweeter literary pictorialism. This is particularly clear in his next complete poem, *The Life and Death of Jason* (1867).

Morris worked at this with his usual formidable energy, sometimes writing as much as seven hundred lines a day. Divided over seventeen books, the poem shows Morris's sheer delight and skill in handling narrative for its own sake and then decorating this with highly pictorial detail. The result is not great drama nor a sense of the primitive and the heroic as much as a fluent and pretty pathos interspersed with moments of lyric that show Morris's metrical deftness:

  But since the golden age is gone,
This little place is left alone,
Unchanged, unchanging, watched of us,
The daughters of wise Hesperus

This sweetly melancholy dream of fair women is part of the song sung by the maidens guarding the Golden Fleece, and this was a theme painted by Burne-Jones at much the same time as the poem was composed. Indeed, Morris's narrative poems were a great influence on Burne-Jones's style as it developed away from the manner of Rossetti towards something altogether more remote and ethereal. Burne-Jones's illustrations to Morris's poems, indeed, were to provide him with images that he was to use throughout the rest of his career.

She reached her hand to him, and with kind eyes
Gazed into his; but he the fingers caught
And drew her to him, and midst ecstasies
Passing all words, yea, well-nigh passing thought,
Felt that sweet breath that he so long had sought,
Felt the warm life within her heaving breast
As in his arms his living love he pressed.

But as his cheek touched hers he heard her say,
"Wilt thou not speak, O love? why dost thou weep?
Art thou then sorry for this long-wished day,
Or dost thou think perchance thou wilt not keep
This that thou holdest, but in dreamy sleep?
Nay, let us do the bidding of the Queen,
And hand in hand walk through thy garden green;

"Then shalt thou tell me, still beholding me,
Full many things whereof I wish to know,
And as we walk from whispering tree to tree
Still more familiar to thee shall I grow,
And such things shalt thou say unto me now
As when thou deemedst thou wast quite alone,
A madman, kneeling to a thing of stone."

This passage from 'Pygmalion and the Image' in The Earthly Paradise *describes the moment when Pygmalion's statue wakes to living flesh. The poem was to have a profound influence on Burne-Jones who twice painted scenes from it.*

It was these qualities of the picturesque and the tender that made *Jason* an immediate success. In an age when narrative poetry was popular, Morris was a master story teller. In *Jason*, he took a Greek legend and told it with the pathos that was then often valued as Chaucer's supreme achievement. In the words of Ernest Rhys, looking back in 1911 to his early enthusiasm for the poem, Morris had found an ancient story and 'reclothed it with the most exquisite pre-Raphaelite draperies, worked upon with all the tints and patterns of the painting, singing, and dreaming middle ages'.

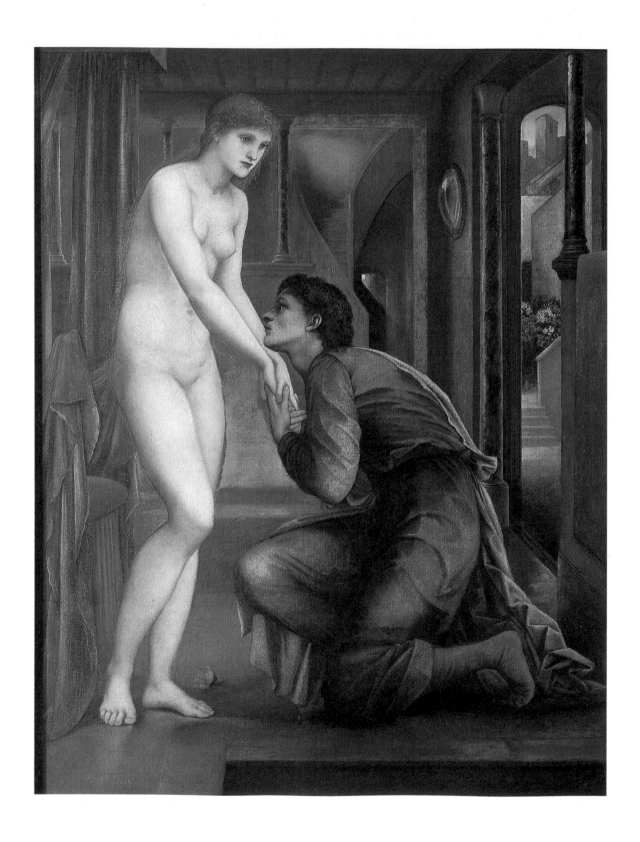

Such poetry was, of course, an escape, an escape from the Victorian city, from the pressure of commercialism and the brute ugliness of the modern world. As such, it was deeply valued. The young Henry James's account of the work in the *North American Review* exactly defines the reasons for Morris's popularity. 'To the jaded intellects of the present moment,' James suggested, 'distracted with the strife of creeds and the conflict of theories, it opens a glimpse into a world where they will be called upon neither to choose, to criticise, nor to believe, but simply to feel, to look, and to listen.'

At the close of *Jason*, Morris himself paid tribute to Chaucer as the poet whose songs, composed amid 'the rose-hung lanes of woody Kent,' survive to soothe a generation entangled in what he calls 'unrejoicing labour'.

It is clear from this tribute that Morris's deep and horrified response to the squalor of Victorian civilisation was becoming ever more central to his thought. The Red House had been a gesture against this, while the products created by the Firm were in open defiance of the shoddiness that characterised much contemporary commercial manufacture.

Morris felt all too keenly that the great upsurge of industrial society, its greed and competition, its blinkered, mercenary demands on a world that it was systematically polluting and degrading, had given rise to a deep spiritual malaise. To Morris as to many Victorians, this fear was both genuine and deep-seated. 'The hope of the past years was gone,' Morris later wrote, 'the struggle of mankind for many ages had produced nothing but this sordid, aimless, ugly confusion; the immediate future seemed likely to intensify all the present evils by sweeping away the last survivals of the days before the dull squalor of civilisation had settled down on the world.'

Jason was designed as a palliative to this. Morris's poetry from this period is thus rooted in his deep awareness of cultural blight, commercial alienation and spiritual loss. Indeed, in the very act of turning its face from these and looking back to the past as a fantasy world, the verse reveals the society in which it was produced. For Morris as a writer there seemed at this time no way of tackling such evils face on. Instead, he saw the function of the poet as being to provide anodynes, to recline in *The Daydreamer* chair and beguile an exhausted but grateful audience.

In the 'Apology' to his next published work, *The Earthly Paradise* (1868–70), this notion of the poet's function becomes much more explicit:

> The heavy trouble, the bewildering care
> That weighs us down who live and earn our bread,
> These idle verses have no power to bear;

Opposite: *Burne-Jones found a constant source of inspiration in Morris's poetry. Morris had versified the tale of Pygmalion in* The Earthly Paradise, *and this picture, entitled* The Soul Attains, *shows the moment when Pygmalion's statue becomes living flesh.*

So let me sing of names remembered,
Because they, living not, can ne'er be dead,
Or long time take their memory quite away
From us poor singers of an empty day.

   Dreamer of dreams, born out of my due time,
Why should I strive to set the crooked straight?
Let it suffice me that my murmuring rhyme
Beats with light wings against the ivory gate,
Telling a tale not too importunate
To those who in the sleepy region stay,
Lulled by the singer of an empty day

'Why should I strive to set the crooked straight?' The question points to the apparent futility of conflict and to the absence of any ideals through which the very real horror of the daily world might be transformed. Better to forget 'the snorting steam and piston stroke' and dream instead 'of London, small, and white, and clean', a medieval London where Geoffrey Chaucer works at the Customs House and spins his incomparable dreams.

The influence of Chaucer and *The Canterbury Tales* is clear in the structure of *The Earthly Paradise*. Just as Chaucer's pilgrims beguile their journey by telling stories, so Morris's travellers, landing on an island where classical and northern traditions are mixed, pass the year by telling the great tales of those two cultures.

The composition of twenty-four verse stories, the writing of 42,000 lines of poetry in six years, was a formidable undertaking. However, although Morris's tales often went through several drafts, there is a limp, excessive length about many of them which is frankly tedious. Versifying was, for Morris, 'a mere matter of craftsmanship,' and there is about his finding of rhymes something of the repetitive monotony of tapestry weaving. For Morris, this was a virtue. 'If a chap can't compose an epic poem while he is weaving a tapestry he had better shut up,' he once declared, and indeed, much of *The Earthly Paradise* was composed in his head while he sat at his design work. Morris would mumble to himself as he drew and then, when the rhymes had been found and the lines appeared fixed, he would rush to his table and write them down.

The prolixity that resulted is aggravated in many of the pieces by a lack of real suffering or development in the characters, by absence of drama in many of the incidents and the reluctance to show real powers of introspection. Nonetheless, there are other qualities which partly offset these limitations, qualities which, despite the often slack vocabulary of the work, disturb the very dream of escapism itself.

There is, first of all, a deep awareness of mortality:

Yea, I have looked and seen November there;
The changeless seal of change it seemed to be,
Fair death of things that, living once, were fair;
Bright sign of loneliness too great for me,
Strange image of the dread eternity,
In whose void patience how can these have part,
These outstretched feverish hands, this restless heart?

Such lines contribute to what the great Morris scholar E.P. Thompson has described in *The Earthly Paradise* as '...an almost mechanical oscillation between sensuous luxury and horror, melancholy and despair'.

The second and increasingly dominant note is of anguish at the failure of love. The 'Lady of the Land', for example, a true Pre-Raphaelite temptress with her golden comb and mirror, naked and with her hair lying back as she dreams 'of some long vanished day', is turned into a dragon at the close of the poem. In 'The Hill of Venus', the lover is tortured by despairing desire:

As though a cold and hopeless tune he heard,
Sung by grey mouths amidst a dull-eyed dream;
Time and again across his heart would stream
The pain of fierce desire whose aim was gone,
Of baffled yearning, loveless and alone.

Love has shown an inner wilderness, and there can be little doubt that such lines reflect Morris's own despair as, in the closing years of the 1860s, his private life collapsed in betrayal. Rossetti, made free by the death of Lizzie Siddal, had returned to claim the woman whom he was now to make into a central figure of the Pre-Raphaelite dream.

Soon after she moved into Queen Square, Jane began to show signs of that neurasthenic withdrawal which was to make much of her adult life so burdensome. Certainly, for periods of time she was in physical pain, having developed problems with her back. In addition, and for all its apparent comfort, her personal life was not a happy one. The move to Queen Square was an undoubted descent in social terms, and Jane was obliged to live there with a man endlessly preoccupied with his business and still subject to alarming fits of rage, a man who loved her nonetheless with an idealising fervour of boyish intensity. This was a passion Jane could not return and which she may have found tedious. Meanwhile, in 1865, Rossetti reappeared and Jane, who had done almost no modelling since her marriage, began to sit for him again and to pose for a series of photographs taken in the garden at Cheyne Walk.

Rossetti's photographs of Jane are among the earliest attempts

Above: *Rossetti was very interested in photography and took a series of portraits of Jane Morris posed in Pre-Raphaelite attitudes. The resulting photographs are eerily poised between art and life.*

Opposite: *Rossetti's portrait of Jane as* La Pia del Tolomei *is one of the most telling and powerful comments on their relationship. The original tale appears in Dante where the lovers are punished for their adultery. Jane is here portrayed as the adulterous woman. In a sketch for the work, the ring with which she fretfully plays was her own wedding ring.*

to catch the muse on film. They have the ghostly intensity of a long dead passion and seem poised between the real woman, beautiful but not flawless, and the artist's ideal of perfection, as Jane stands withdrawn in a silence of dangerous, cold allure. This is indeed the woman Henry James described.

Rossetti—burly, besuited, bullish in speech and relishing the latest English slang—still maintained much of his youthful magnetism. His hair was richly brown, his square-trimmed beard slightly lighter. His olive skinned face was both thoughtful yet sensual while, from behind his spectacles, there peered his blue-grey eyes.

They peered particularly at Jane whose image he was now beginning to work ever more powerfully into his art. In *The Merciless Lady* she appears as the figure drawing him away from an earlier and now dead affair. She looks on as two men struggle in *A Fight for a Woman*. By 1868, it seems that Rossetti had won that fight and the couple were seeing each other regularly. They have become *Tristram and Yseult Drinking the Love Potion*, while, with more subtle allusion, Jane is *La Pia de Tolomei* in one of Rossetti's greatest canvasses.

In the *Purgatorio*, La Pia is the wife of a cruel husband who imprisons her in the fortress where she dies. In Rossetti's painting, she is Jane Morris imprisoned in a hateful marriage. Rooks caw over the wintery landscape, while the lady, withdrawn in her suffering, plays with the ring on her hand until her knuckles whiten. In an early sketch for the work, that ring was Jane's own wedding ring.

The 'jolly' surface of life was maintained. In April 1868, Rossetti threw a lavish dinner party to celebrate his work on *La Pia*. Both Morris and Jane attended. Henry James, who met Morris at this time, found him an impressive figure. 'He is short, burly, corpulent, very careless and unfinished in his dress,' he wrote. 'He has a very loud voice and a nervous restless manner and a perfectly unaffected and business-like address. His talk is wonderfully to the point and remarkable for clear good sense. . . He's an extraordinary example, in short, of a delicate sensitive genius and taste, saved by a perfectly healthy body and temper.'

But if this was the appearance Morris showed to the world, his inner anguish at Jane's withdrawal of love was intensely painful. This is reflected in some poems he never published in his lifetime but which are amongst the finest of his works. They are charged with a personal directness, a spare and sometimes excruciating honesty. This is particularly true of the unfinished 'Why Dost Thou Struggle.'

Why dost thou struggle, strive for victory
Over my heart that loveth thine so well?
When Death shall one day have its will of thee
And to deaf ears thy triumph thou must tell.

Unto deaf ears or unto such as know
The hearts of dead and living wilt thou say:

*This unfinished poem is a
moving analysis of Morris's
relationship with his wife, a
profoundly honest piece of self-
revelation.*

'A childish heart there loved me once and lo
I took his love and cast his love away.

'A childish greedy heart! yet still he clung
So close to me that much he pleased my pride
And soothed a sorrow that about me hung
With glimpses of his love unsatisfied . . .

'But now my heart grown silent of its grief
Saw more than kindness in his hungry eyes
But I must wear a mask of false belief
And feign that nought I know his miseries.

'I wore a mask because though certainly
I loved him not yet was there something soft
And sweet to have him ever loving me
Belike it is I well nigh loved him oft—

'Nigh loved him oft and needs must grant to him
Some kindness out of all he asked of me
And hoped his love would still hang vague, dim,
About my life like half-heard melody.

'He knew my heart and over-well knew this
And strove poor soul to pleasure me herein;
But yet what might he do? some doubtful kiss,
Some word, some look might give him hope to win.

'Poor hope, poor soul, for he again would come
Thinking to gain yet one more golden step
Toward love's shrine and lo! the kind speech dumb
The kind look gone, no love upon my lip—

'Yea gone, yet not my fault. I knew of love,
But my love and not his; nor could I tell
That such blind passion in him I should move.
Behold, I have loved faithfully and well!'

'Love of my love so deep and measureless
O Lords of the new world this too ye know

(unfinished)

The poem opens with the man's bitterness at the woman's assertion of power over him, a power exercised despite the fact she knows she has his heart in thrall. Then, remarkably, the verses become the woman's soliloquy, her view of the affair. We see Morris as he imagines Jane seeing him. Both characters become figures of great pathos as the poet's analysis unfolds.

The woman recognises the boyish innocence in the man's love and confesses how she has exploited this and trampled on it. The greediness of the boy is suggested, but so also is the woman's pride in her power. She has used the man's love, she realises, to hide her own deeper distress and because it has something easy and appealing in it. But there was no true depth of passion. Now that the woman has deeply hurt the man, she dare not offer any consolation. The pained boy must be kept at a distance so that he is not hurt more, while, in this very separation, the woman begins to glimpse her own callousness. Pathos belongs to each of these divided characters—to the man in his spoilt naivety and the woman in her irresponsibility. The lines have the terse but all-inclusive simplicity of a great tragic affair. Morris himself could not complete the poem, but in the greatest tale from *The Earthly Paradise*, 'The Lovers of Gudrun', he was able to transform this personal pathos into considerable narrative art.

'The Lovers of Gudrun' is taken from the Icelandic *Laxdaela Saga*, one of the most romantic of these great works. It culminates in a tragic love triangle which, in Morris's words: '. . . shows how two friends loved a fair woman, and how he who loved her best had her to wife, though she loved him little or not at all.' The parallel to Morris's own situation is painfully clear, while his handling of the great dramatic climaxes is more than usually effective.

The original saga is shot through with religious learning and a feeling for history, with a love of old heroic poetry and the new courtly literature of the thirteenth century. There is much emphasis on the glory of great occasions and on tableaux, while the tragic love triangle of Kjartan, Bodli and the imperious, vengefully passionate Gudrun, is one of the great achievements of saga literature.

Morris himself was aiming at a recreation rather than an accurate transcription. Many of his changes are distinctly Pre-Raphaelite in the glowing detail and melancholic self-pity with which they soften the terse moral objectivity of the original. Gudrun, for example, is often seen as a maiden in the Burne-Jones style, ivory necked and with the wind playing in her luxurious hair, but the blind and ageing heroine, pressed by her son to say which of the men in her life she loved the most, achieves a dignified pathos in her reply:

> She turned, until her sightless eyes did gaze
> As though the wall, the hills, must melt away.
> And show her Herdholt in the twilight grey;
> She cried, with tremulous voice, and eyes grown wet
> For the last time, whate'er should happen yet,
> With hands stretched out for all that she had lost:
> 'I did the worst to him I loved the most.'

Something of the inexorable tragedy and mysterious depth of the original has been retained.

Morris himself was well aware that 'The Lovers of Gudrun' was the best tale in *The Earthly Paradise*. He wrote to Swinburne (who had privately expressed some reservations about 'the *trailing* style of the work') how he was painfully conscious 'that the book would have done me more credit if there had been nothing in it but the Gudrun, though I don't think the others quite the worst things I have done. Yet they are all too long and flabby, damn it!'

While a modern reader is almost certain to agree, the success of *The Earthly Paradise* was very considerable. It was expressly designed to soothe the cares of the age and in this it succeeded admirably. For all the enormous range of his activities and his far greater success in other fields, during his lifetime Morris was for many the poet of *The Earthly Paradise*.

The book was also to have one admirer of exceptional importance. During 1868 there appeared in the *Westminster Review* an unsigned essay on all of Morris's poetry to date. The writer of the piece found in the poems what so many responded to: '. . . the continual suggestion, pensive or passionate, of the shortness of life; this is contrasted to the bloom of the world and gives new seductions to it; the sense of death and the desire of beauty; the desire of beauty quickened by the sense of death.'

In a world where philosophy has, it is alleged, shown the inconstancy and changefulness of all things and so left man bewildered and alone, only heightened and prolonged sensation of the type Morris provided could show life at its fullest. 'To burn always with this hard and gem-like flame, to maintain this ecstasy, is success in life,' the writer declared. The great means of achieving this state is art 'for art comes to you professing frankly to give nothing but the highest quality to your moments as they pass, and simply for the moment's sake'. When Walter Pater transferred these famous sentences to the conclusion of *The Renaissance* in 1873, he gave Oscar Wilde and his contemporaries one of their sacred texts. Pater's meditation on *The Earthly Paradise* is thus one of the foundations of the Aesthetic Movement of the 1890s.

This was not the path Morris himself was to tread, however. His own valuation of his work was far more modest than that which Pater advanced. Instead, he had turned to a deeper study of the Icelandic sources of his best tale and so progressed from being the 'idle singer of an empty day' towards becoming the advocate of what he was later to call the 'religion of courage'. Iceland and the spirit of the sagas was to play a vital role in this.

A life scarce worth the living, a poor fame
Scarce worth the winning, in a wretched land,
Where fear and pain go upon either hand,
As toward the end men fare without an aim
Unto the dull grey dark from whence they came:
Let them alone, the unshadowed sheer rocks stand
Over the twilight graves of that poor band,
Who count so little in the great world's game!

Nay, with the dead I deal not; this man lives,
And that which carried him through good and ill,
Stern against fate while his voice echoed still
From rock to rock, now he lies silent, strives
With wasting time, and through its long lapse gives
Another friend to me, life's void to fill.

Morris's Prefatory Sonnet to
The Story of Grettir the Strong *describes the heroism of the Icelandic sagas that was such a profound source of consolation to him in his period of deepest unhappiness.*

To read the sagas required a knowledge of the language in which they had originally been composed. In the autumn of 1868, Warrington Taylor had introduced Morris to Eirikr Magnusson. The two men had a close physical resemblance and were soon to become fast friends. They agreed to read Icelandic with each other three times a week and began with the saga of *Gunnlaug the Wormtongue*. Morris, with characteristic impetuosity, realised that grammar learning would slow down matters severely. 'You be my grammar as we go along,' he told Magnusson. In this way they could start translating at once.

Magnusson himself described their method of working. 'We went together over every day's task as carefully as the eager-mindedness of the pupil to acquire the story would allow. I afterwards wrote out at home a literal translation of it and handed it to him at our next lesson. With this before him Morris wrote down at his leisure his own version in his own style, which ultimately did service as printer's copy when the Saga was published.' In this way, the translation of *Gunnlaug the Wormtongue* (1869) was finished in a fortnight. Translations of *The Grettis Saga* and *The Laxdaela Saga* followed in rapid succession during the same year.

Once again, Morris brought originality to his work, although, in the words of Magnusson, 'His style is a subject on which there exists considerable diversity of opinion'. What Morris was determined to avoid was the style his daughter May later called Magnusson's 'unconsidered journalese'. While this might have been a desirable aim, Morris's own attempt to create a medieval Norse flavour has much of the irksomeness of the fake antique. Phrases of Magnusson's such as 'it happened' and 'King Ethelred was sorely bewildered' are far more effective than Morris's 'it betid' and 'King Ethelred was mickle mind-sick.' For all Morris's praise of *The Volsung Saga* as 'the great Story of the North which should be to all our race what the Tale of Troy was to the Greeks,' his style makes his translation exceptionally tedious. In about 1870 however Morris prepared a finely illuminated manuscript version of the saga, and it is to his work in calligraphy and illustration we should now turn.

Morris's principal work in these fields was crammed into a mere six years. It reveals a rapid and interesting development as well as growing technical expertise and scholarship.

Morris had begun illumination as early as 1856. None of these experiments unfortunately survives, though their use of a Gothic script, of decorated borders and rich initials, won the great approval of both Rossetti and Ruskin. When Morris returned to illumination in 1870, it was with *A Book of Verse*, a collaborative exercise by Burne-Jones, Fairfax Murray, George Wardle and Morris himself.

This is a lovely book: fresh, light and natural. The lettering is Roman and was possibly taken from the early sixteenth century Italian manuals on handwriting Morris is known to have owned. His calligraphy was to develop—not without some awkward experiments such as the uninteresting lettering of *The Dwellers at Eyr*—until, in the 'Odes of Horace', he achieved a light italic hand which is very pleasing. These experiments were also to be highly influential since they were to impress those who later guided Edward Johnstone, the great modern pioneer of revised calligraphy. The illumination of these manuscripts also shows a considerable range of experiment. The manuscript of *The Story of the Volsungs and the Niblungs*, for example offers pages lightly powdered with restrained plant motifs and figures. By 1872, Morris's illumination was being more and more guided by his historical research into both design and technique. He began to mix his paints with white of egg and, with the 'Omar Khayyam', to work on vellum with a proliferation of gilded foliage that tends to be somewhat heavy. His last completed experiment, the 'Odes of Horace', is clearly influenced by French and Italian examples of the later fifteenth century. The initial letters are richly decorated with motifs that Renaissance scribes had adopted from Romanesque manuscripts, while in the curling patterns of acanthus leaves the formal has to a large extent replaced the naturalistic.

It was during these years that Morris and Burne-Jones also produced some of their most remarkable stained glass windows, works which, at their best glow with an almost incandescent celebration of the glazier's art.

These windows represent a triumph of cooperative design and the skills developed by Morris's glass painters under the expert

Opposite: A Book of Verse *was illuminated for Georgina Burne-Jones and was Morris's first mature experiment in this medium. It has great charm and freshness and is largely devoid of the historicist influences that characterize Morris's later illuminated work.*

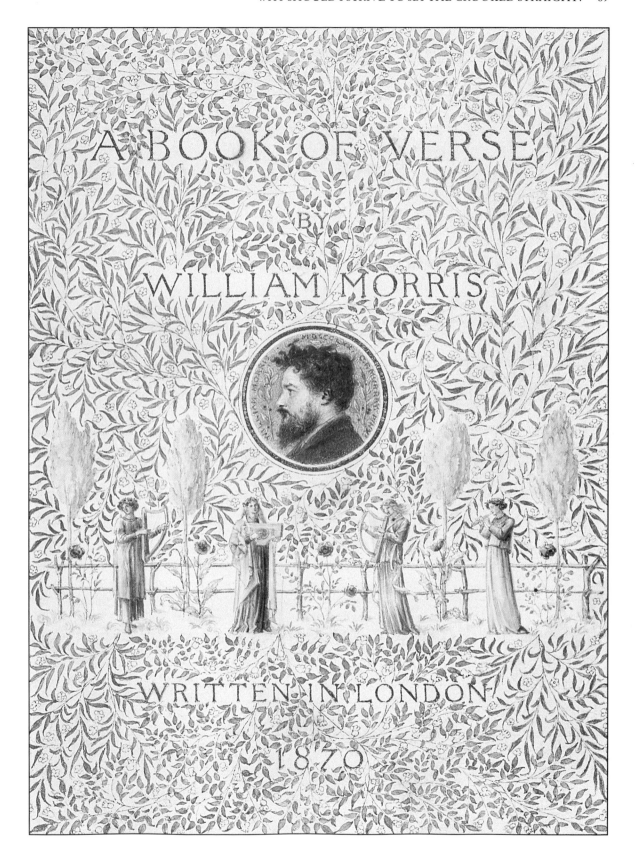

guidance of both George Campfield and Morris. In rivalling the work of some of the great medieval masters, they suggest Morris's wisdom and skill in setting up his studio in imitation of the medieval system of workshop production where numerous talents combined in the making of a single work.

The glass studio at Queen Square housed a motley crew of Pre-Raphaelite geniuses, highly trained artisans, family friends and lads from a boys' home on the Euston Road. Under the all-pervasive influence of Morris, however, the works fulfilled an ideal which he was later to express in one of his lectures:

Above: *The window in the South aisle of St Mary's church, King's Walden, Hertfordshire is a fine example of the Firm's work in this medium.*

Opposite: *A page from Morris's illuminated manuscript of Horace's* Odes, *1876. It shows his work in this medium at its most florid.*

> . . . the handicraftsman, left behind by the artist when the arts
> sundered, must come up with him, must work side by side with
> him: apart from the differences between a great master and a
> scholar, apart from the natural differences of the bent of men's
> minds, which would make one man an imitative, and another an
> architectural or decorative artist, there should be no difference
> between those employed on strictly ornamental work; and the
> body of artists dealing with this should quicken with their art all
> makers of things into artists also.

Before work could begin at all, templates of the original window lights had to be drawn and cut, figures, borders and canopies discussed in terms of the overall scheme, and a cartoon commissioned if fresh designs were to be used. When the cartoon had been drawn, Morris gave detailed instructions to Campfield about the colours to be employed. He also often designed the positioning of the leads which held the mosaics in place. The various parts of the window were then distributed to the painters whose work he closely supervised. Morris suggested retouching where he considered this necessary and the glass was then fired and leaded up. 'When this was done,' Mackail records, 'there came the final review of the window, a work of great difficulty in any case, and to any ordinary eye impossible in the cramped premises of Queen Square, where some of the largest windows were made. But here his amazing eye and memory for colour enabled him to achieve the impossible: he could pass all the parts of a large window one by one before the light, and never lose sight of the general tone of the colour or of the relation of one part to another. If any part did not satisfy him, new glass was cut and that piece of the window done again.'

This is a vivid picture of a mastercraftsman in action, wholly absorbed in the practical and aesthetic considerations of his work. The best of the windows Morris was preparing in this way are also among the most remarkable achievements of Victorian art. There are, for example, the three lancets of the east window in the South Aisle of St Michael's, Tilehurst, Berkshire where the attendant angels play their instruments against a thrilling background of powdered stars.

Even more impressive are the three angels blowing long trumpets from the church of St Edward the Confessor, Cheddleton, Staffordshire. The robes, of these figures sway and flutter with a liveliness not always to be seen in Burne-Jones's work as they turn inwards to the central figure. But it is Morris's use of a many-hued silver stain on a white glass for these robes and the magnificent relation of this to the red of the angels' wings that is the most exhilarating achievement. The angels seem to burn with a seraphic majesty made all the more intense by the pale blue of the trefoils above, in which plants shoot up with astonishing energy.

Left: *These three angels from the East window of the South aisle of St Michael's church, Tilehurst, Berkshire were painted in 1869. They are among the supreme achievements of the Firm's stained glass manufacture. The colour has a thrilling intensity and variety, a true sense of something other-worldly and powerful.*

In All Saints', Middleton Cheney, that fire is finally kindled, for here are Shadrach, Meshach and Abednego, cool in their grey-blues as the orange and yellow flames of the fiery furnace—drawn with a linear energy prefiguring *art nouveau*—rage about them.

Yet even as Burne-Jones's style developed, so he began to lose contact for a while with the medieval principles of two dimensional glass design. His *Transfiguration* from St Cuthbert's, Lytham, already suggests the pictorial illusion that can be seen again in the Easthampstead 'Last Judgement'. The drama here is undeniable and the figure of the Pantocrator in the roundel has elegance if not force. The dominant whites and reds—the silver St Michael and the red-winged, white-robed angels; the pale rising dead and the risen blessed—contribute greatly to this effect. But there is again a suggested illusion of painted space, an emphasis which can be seen again in *The Rivers of Paradise* window, designed for All Hallows, Allerton, Liverpool, where some of Burne-Jones's later glasswork can also be seen. These last windows are in a wholly different manner, however, sumptuous in their colour but expressionistic in the rhythms of their leads especially.

A masterpiece such as the *Last Judgement*, West Window in St Philip's Cathedral, Birmingham, points forward to the experiments of the twentieth century and is a long way from those sources of inspiration which between 1869 and 1875 allowed Morris and Burne-Jones to produce some of the greatest works of the Victorian Gothic revival.

While Morris was involved in this extraordinary range of activities, the affair between Jane and Rossetti dragged on, bringing pain to all three of them. Indeed, in 1869, Jane's health had sunk so low that Morris felt it his duty to take her for a cure to Bad-Ems in Hesse-Nassau. Here Rossetti sent Jane a cartoon which shows her reclining in a bath with seven glasses of spa water in front of her and Morris behind her, reading from the seven volumes of *The Earthly Paradise*. The implication is that the one is as distasteful as the other.

Below: The Fiery Furnace *from All Saints' Church, Middleton Cheney, Northamptonshire is one of the most dramatic windows ever produced by the Firm.*

But if Rossetti could joke at the situation he could also bring to it the moral blackmail of the hopelessly obsessed. In his letters, he tried to shift his destruction of Morris's marriage onto the plain of high idealism. 'All that concerns you is the all-absorbing question with me,' he wrote to Jane, suggesting that Morris would not mind him telling her this. 'The more he loves you,' he continued, 'the more he knows that you are too lovely and noble not to be loved: and, dear Janey, there are too few things that seem worth expressing as life goes on, for one friend to deny another the poor expression of what is most at his heart.' Morris, in other words, was to surrender his wife to his master.

This is the suggestion of a man on the brink of a nervous breakdown, and Rossetti's poems from this period reveal the agonised depth of a reciprocated but illicit passion. The painful confusion of Morris's position is revealed by the fact that when Rossetti's volume of work was published, Morris himself reviewed it for *The Academy*. The sonnets written in passionate adoration of his own wife, he compared to Shakespeare's 'for depth of thought, and skill and felicity of execution'.

The king, it seemed, had won the game of courtly love. His victory, however, had cost him his health. 'It was hoped,' Mackail wrote, 'that quiet life in a remote country house might do much to restore him.' To this end, Rossetti and Morris agreed to share the rent of £60 a year on Kelmscott Manor, an Oxfordshire farmhouse of the sixteenth and seventeenth centuries.

For Morris, Kelmscott had the beauty and magic of a dream. Fields and water and Cotswold stone seemed to realise the ideal of man's dignified life in harmony with nature. Much later he was to write how '. . . through its south window you not only catch a glimpse of the Thames clover meadows and the pretty little elm-crowned hill over in Berkshire, but if you sit in the proper place, you can see not only the barn . . . with its beautiful sharp gable, the grey stone sheds, and the dove-cot, but also the flank of the earlier house and its little gables and grey scaled roofs'.

Below: *A watercolour of Kelmscott Manor, the house in Oxfordshire which was Morris's retreat from London and where for part of the year Jane lived with Rossetti.*

In this passage from News from Nowhere, *Morris's deep love for Kelmscott Manor is apparent.*

'Yes, friend, this is what I came out for to see; this many-gabled old house built by the simple country-folk of the long-past times, regardless of all the turmoil that was going on in cities and courts, is lovely still amidst all the beauty which these latter days have created: and I do not wonder at our friends tending it carefully and making much of it. It seems to me as if it had waited for these happy days, and held in it the gathered crumbs of happiness of the confused and turbulent past.'

She led me up close to the house, and laid her shapely sun browned hand and arm on the lichened wall as if to embrace it, and cried out, 'O me! O me! How I love the earth, and the seasons, and weather, and all things that deal with it, and all that grows out of,—as this has done!'

Yet for the early years of his tenancy, Kelmscott was a dreamland Morris could only rarely enter. Rossetti turned the Tapestry Room into his studio and moved in his dogs, his furniture and his mistress. Jane flourished in her husband's absence, went for long walks, modelled for Rossetti and became the muse of his sonnet cycle in *The House of Life*.

But if this was a creative and even happy period for him, Kelmscott was not Rossetti's true spiritual home. He was thoroughly a man of the city, hated the discomforts of the house and loathed its winter coldness. He was an alien, self-torturing presence there, and Morris, with his deep affinity for the English countryside, resented this as bitterly as anything else. In a letter to Mrs Coronio, one of those women who, with Georgina Burne-Jones, helped to sustain him through this agonising time, he wrote:

> . . . Rossetti has set himself down at Kelmscott as if he never meant to go away; and not only does that keep me from that harbour of refuge (because it is really a farce our meeting when we can help it) but also he has all sorts of ways so unsympathetic with the sweet simple old place, that I feel his presence there as a kind of slur on it.

There is in this resentful outburst a feeling of spiritual trespass, and Morris, emotionally wounded and deprived of his true 'harbour of refuge' now sought out his other spiritual home, the wild, hard coasts of Iceland. Tormented, he would embrace the storm and find new courage:

Ah! shall Winter mend your case?
Set your teeth the wind to face.

Beat the snow, tread down the frost!
All is gained when all is lost.

Morris set out for Iceland early in June 1871. He took with him as his companions his old Oxford friend Charles Faulkner, Eiríkr Magnusson, his fellow translator of the sagas, and W. H. Evans, an army officer who came along for the fishing and shooting. They were four men from the upper middle classes in the richest country in Europe and were now going to one of the continent's poorest and most backward lands. The expedition was to be a challenge to their stamina, to their sense of adventure and their ability to absorb cultural contrasts.

For Morris, this contact with a landscape that was by turns hard, dismal and exhilarating was profoundly important. The 'idle singer' was challenged into the new sense of realism shown in the journal of his expedition. The artificial prose of the Icelandic translations has gone and in its place is something forthright but vivid and even on occasions humorous. Morris's alternations of mood, his sense of excitement and the undertow of despair are both recorded. He gives a vivid sense of his own physical robustness, his outbursts of temper and also of a new stoicism born of exertion and memories of the sagas. 'A piece of turf under your feet, and the sky overhead, that's all: whatever solace your life is to have must come out of yourself or these old stories, not over-hopeful themselves.'

We turned a corner of the stony stepped grey hills, and below us lay a deep calm sound, say two miles broad, a hog-backed steep mountain-island forming the other side of it, next to which lay a steeper islet, a mere rock; and then other islands, the end of which we could not see, entangled the sound and swallowed it up; I was most deeply impressed with it all, yet can scarcely tell you why; it was like nothing I had ever seen, but strangely like my old imaginations of places for sea-wanderers to come to: the day was quite a hot summer day now, and there was no cloud in the sky and the atmosphere was very, very clear, but a little pillowy cloud kept dragging and always changing yet always there over the top of the little rocky islet . . . All the islands, whether sloping or sheer rocks, went right into the sea without a handsbreadth of beach anywhere; and, little thing as that seems, I suppose it is this which gives the air of romanticism to these strange islands. Close by the sea lay the many gables (black wood with green turf roofs) of the farm of Kirkinbœ (Kirkby), a little white-washed church being the nearest to the sea, while close under the basalt cliff was the ruin of a stone mediaeval church: a most beautiful and poetical place it looked to me, but more remote and

Morris's Journal of his first trip to Iceland has a directness that is only rarely found in his descriptive writing.

melancholy than I can say, in spite of the flowers and grass and
bright sun: it looked as if you might live for a hundred years
before you would ever see ship sailing into the bay there; as if the
old life of the saga-time had gone, and the modern life had never
reached the place.

But if a hard landscape and an unselfpitying literature were a
'good corrective to the maundering side of medievalism,' the Icelandic people also impressed him. Poor yet contented, humorous
and brave, they were wholly different to the men and women
caught up in the complexity and insidious divisiveness of English
social life. They impressed Morris unforgettably and were a
crucial influence on his maturing thought. Looking back on his
Icelandic experiences twelve years later he wrote: 'I learned one
lesson there, thoroughly I hope, that the most grinding poverty is
a trifling evil compared to the inequality of the classes.' The social
reformer was being born and a new strength was being found.
When, at the end of the year, Morris wrote to Mrs Coronio of a
second visit he was preparing to Iceland, he reflected on what a
blessing his first visit had been and 'what horrors it saved me
from'.

Domestic affairs were now indeed progressing to a crisis. Rossetti's poetry had been attacked for its alleged immorality in three
important magazines, and in May 1872 Robert Buchanan
reissued his notorious attack 'The Fleshly School of Poetry' in
pamphlet form. The poet himself, already in a torment of guilt,
was now plagued by insomnia for which he took large doses of
chloral and whisky.

Eventually, he tried to commit suicide but survived only
to suffer a schizophrenic breakdown. He was plagued by
hallucinations and fears of conspiracy. Nonetheless, by the end
of September he was back at Kelmscott and was beginning to
sketch Jane as Proserpine, the mortal imprisoned with the king of
the underworld for half the year, even as Jane was obliged to
spend the winters in London with her husband.

Morris's letters to Mrs Coronio show how he was very slowly
advancing towards an acceptance of the situation. This was by no
means easy or straightforward. In October 1872 Morris could
write that 'on the whole I suppose I am getting rather less restless
and worried, if at the same time less hopeful'. The following
month, however, he made clear that he considered the collapse of
the marriage to be a personal failure. His letter, indeed, is a
shrewd piece of self-analysis:

. . . to have real friends and some sort of an aim in life is so much,
that I ought still to think myself lucky: and often in my better

moods I wonder what it is in me that throws me into such a rage and despair at other times. I suspect, do you know, that some such moods would have come upon me at times even without this failure of mine.

A spring trip to Italy with Burne-Jones still found him restive. The second visit to Iceland was a success, but by the end of 1873 Morris was vowing to take up figure drawing again, hoping its very difficulty would be a palliative.

At Kelmscott, matters were rapidly deteriorating, and in 1874 Morris took Jane to Belgium, principally perhaps to get her away from her lover. Rossetti's insanity was now becoming dangerous. While strolling with his doctor he believed he had been insulted by a party of local fishermen. He turned and overwhelmed them with abuse. Village gossip rose to a crescendo and it was decided that Rossetti should leave Kelmscott for good.

These years of personal suffering were also a period of great creative achievement for Morris. Indeed, they show his flowering into the greatest of all English masters of pattern design. Nowhere is this more evident than in the series of wallpapers he created between 1872 and 1876.

Morris's Willow *paper of c. 1874 (***below left***) is one of his freshest and most appealing designs and was created with the most subtle interplay of rhythms. These bind the design together without ever impinging on its naturalness.* Larkspur *(***below right***) is a more geometric working of similar ideas.*

The best of these have a lightness and freshness which has been widely praised, and their naturalism is indeed exquisite. The *Willow* of 1874 has a rhythm so delicate that it ranks as one of Morris's finest creations: joyous yet chaste, while showing a directional emphasis that is so subtley hidden as to be barely noticeable. *Jasmine* is perhaps a little pallid, but *Larkspur*, just suggesting depth without becoming illusionistic, is a deft combination of frontally facing full blooms and irises seen from the side. The flowers repeat in miniature the swirls of the leaves that run from the central, sinuous stalk. When actually decorating a room, the paper is again a highly successful piece of design since the horizontal accents form a lively contrast to the bands of coloured flowers. Later, under the influence of textiles seen in the Victoria and Albert Museum, Morris was to develop such ideas into some of his finest mature designs.

Morris also continued to write poetry with varied success. *Love is Enough* (1872) is an enervated drama in the mode of the medieval Interlude. It centres around King Pharamond's pursuit and loss of a beautiful girl glimpsed in a vision. While metrically various—the result of considerable labour on Morris's part—the work is not on the whole a success. Indeed, the chief interest of the project lies paradoxically in the binding of the book which is the finest Morris produced. The single band of interlaced gold willow leaves has a light but richly stylised naturalism and a most satisfying relationship with the lettering. Morris was not to develop this interest much further however, preferring in later life covers that were 'rough'. He even suggested to Cobden-Sanderson, the great pioneer of modern book-binding, that a machine could do the job perfectly satisfactorily.

Morris's interest in the epic resulted in a relatively undistinguished translation of the *Aeneid*, published in 1875 and subsequently partly illustrated. His involvement in saga literature however reached its apogee with the publication of *Sigurd the Volsung* in 1876.

Morris had published a prose version of this five years earlier and had a keen appreciation of the true qualities of the work. As he wrote to a friend: 'The scene of the last interview between Sigurd and the despairing and terrible Brynhild touches me more than anything I have ever met with in literature; there is nothing wanting in it, nothing forgotten, nothing repeated, nothing over-strained; all tenderness is shown without the use of a tender word, all misery and despair without a word of raving, complete beauty without an ornament, and all this in two pages of moderate print.'

Morris's own version of the tale is a skilful reworking of the many and complex sources in which the events are recounted. The surviving manuscripts also show the very considerable

Above: *The cover of* Love is Enough.

labour he put into perfecting the chief scenes. The result is by far the best of his verse narratives and has a genuine claim to literary importance. Mackail thought the work the most Homeric poem since the *Odyssey*, while Alfred Noyes described it as an '. . . unending sea of song, swelling and dying and surging again like the wind in some mighty primaeval pine-wood'. Morris's portrayal of the passions unleashed by the story has a primitive force unmatched elsewhere in his verse and this is equalled by his powers of characterisation and ability to describe action. Brynhild in particular moves through the work with awe-inspiring majesty. *Sigurd*, however, did not have the success Morris had enjoyed with *The Earthly Paradise* and he was to write little more verse of any importance. As Henry James shrewdly observed, Morris's poetry was 'only his sub-trade'. His real business, as James fully recognised, was the work of the Firm.

This passage from Sigurd the Volsung *suggests the considerable poetic power of his work.*

There now is Brynhild abiding as a Queen in the house of the
  Kings,
And hither and thither she wendeth through the day of queenly
  things;
And no man knoweth her sorrow; though whiles is the Niblung
  bed
Too hot and weary a dwelling for the temples of her head,
And she wends, as her wont was aforetime, when the moon is
  riding high,
And the night on the earth is deepest; and she deemeth it good to
  lie
In the trench of the windy mountains, and the track of the
  wandering sheep,
While soft in the arms of Sigurd Queen Gudrun lieth asleep:
There she cries on the lovely Sigurd, and she cries on the love
  and the oath,
And she cries on the change and vengeance, and the death to
  deliver them both
But her crying none shall hearken, and her sorrow nought shall
  know,
Save the heart of the golden Sigurd, and the man fast bound in
  woe: . . .

But of Gunnar the Niblung they say it, that the bloom of his
  youth is o'er,
And many are manhood's troubles, and they burden him oft and
  sore.
He dwells with Brynhild his wife, with Grimhild his mother he
  dwells,
And noble things of his greatness, of his joy, the rumour tells;
Yet oft and oft of an even he thinks of the tale of the night,
And the shame springs fresh in his heart at his brother Sigurd's
  might;
And the wonder riseth within him, what deed did Sigurd there,
What gift to the King hath he given: and he looks on Brynhild the
  fair,

Opposite: *A portrait of Morris by G. F. Watts, 1870.*

The fair face never smiling, and the eyes that know no change,
And he deems in the bed of the Niblungs she is but cold and
    strange;
And the Lie is laid between them, as the sword lay awhile
    agone . . .

In the hall sitteth Sigurd by Brynhild, in the council of the Kings,
And he hearkeneth her spoken wisdom, and her word of lovely
    things:
In the field they meet, and the wild-wood, on the acre and the
    heath;
And scarce may he tell if the meeting be worse than the coward's
    death,
Or better than life of the righteous: but his love is a flaming fire,
That hath burnt up all before it of the things that feed desire.

The heart of Gudrun he seeth, her heart of burning love,
That knoweth of nought but Sigurd on the earth, in the heavens
    above,
Save the foes that encompass his life, and the woman that wasteth
    away
'Neath the toils of a love like her love, and the unrewarded day:
For hate her eyes hath quickened, and no more is Gudrun blind,
And sure, though dim it may be, she seeth the days behind:
And the shadowy wings of the Lie, that the hand unwitting led
To the love and the heart of Gudrun, brood over board and bed;
And for all the hand of the hero and the foresight of the wise,
From the heart of a loving woman shall the death of men arise.

This was now expanding so rapidly that in 1873 Morris and his family had been obliged to move out of Queen Square and into Horrington House in what was then the pleasantly rural area of Chiswick Lane in West London. Two years later, with business still increasing but with the need to supplement his falling share income, Morris decided to reconstitute the Firm under his sole management.

This major move was a recognition of the true state of affairs, though it was not effected without acrimony. By 1874, Rossetti, Maddox Brown, Marshall and Faulkner were effectively sleeping partners. Morris, assisted by George Wardle, bore the burden of organisation and, along with Webb and Burne-Jones, produced the greater part of the designs as well. Marshall and Maddox Brown were nonetheless outraged and sought legal advice. Their solicitor tried to argue that since at its inception all the partners in the Firm had been rewarded for their work and investment at an agreed rate, 'The position of the several members ought to be considered as equal in respect of their claims on the assets of the firm'. This was quite unrealistic in view of the way the business had developed and would also have entailed a capital depreciation of some seven or eight thousand pounds. Webb, Faulkner and Burne-Jones waived their claims, but Brown, Marshall and Rossetti stuck to their guns. In the event, they were obliged to settle for £1000 each.

Maddox Brown vowed he would never willingly speak to Morris again. Rossetti, having ensured that his settlement was set aside for Jane, retreated with her to the South Coast where he was working on his most magnificent evocation of her allure: the *Astarte Syriaca*. This picture is an extraordinarily powerful vision of the Eternal Feminine whose worship had reduced him to insanity. 'That Gabriel *was* mad was but too true,' Jane wrote after his death in 1882, adding: 'no-one knows it better than myself.'

Rossetti and Morris were also estranged while Jane was distanced from both. Though much of the rest of her life was to be spent in valetudinarian withdrawal, Morris was about to enter a period of the most astonishing activity. Master of his own business, a designer of increasing greatness and variety, he was also to find that he was no longer content to be 'the idle singer of an empty day'. The dreamer of dreams was waking to the full and painful reality of the world about him and he was soon to commit his Titan's energies to striving to set the crooked straight.

BUSINESSMAN, DESIGNER AND CRITIC

In April 1876, soon after becoming sole proprietor of the newly reconstituted Firm, Morris opened a shop at the corner of Oxford Street and North Audley Street, then the most fashionable shopping area in London. The premises were run in a business-like manner, probably by the Smith brothers who were later to become partners.

In the Oxford Street shop, customers were shown a range of pattern-books, photographs, sketches and completed products. Orders, once placed, were then transmitted to the various manufacturing premises. While Queen Square continued for some time to be the most important of these, curtain-making and upholstery were carried out in nearby Granville Place, along with tapestry conservation.

Morris and Co were clearly offering a wide range of goods to their customers, and the opening of the Oxford Street shop marks a convenient point from which to survey production between 1876 and the early 1880s. This included designs for printed and woven textiles, for wallpapers, carpets, tapestries and embroideries, as well as the entire interior decorative schemes in which these items were used. Such a range of activity was not only a demanding business enterprise, it also reveals Morris's continuing innovation, his search for quality, and his deepening criticism of the standards of the commercial world about him. In the entrepreneur lay the seeds of the radical.

Opposite: Strawberry Thief, *dating from 1883, was one of the most popular fabrics on sale at Morris's new shop in Oxford Street. Despite the commercial nature of the business, Morris continued to experiment with textile printing techniques; in this case the indigo discharge method.*

People say to me often enough: If you want to make your art succeed and flourish, you must make it the fashion: a phrase which I confess annoys me; for they mean by it that I should spend one day over my work to two days in trying to convince rich, and supposed influential people, that they care very much for what they really do not care in the the least, so that it may happen according to the proverb: *Bell-wether took the leap, and we all went over.* Well, such advisers are right if they are content with the thing lasting but a little while; say till you can make a

This passage from The Lesser Arts *suggests the integrity with which Morris pursued his aims.*

little money—if you don't get pinched by the door shutting too
quickly: otherwise they are wrong: the people they are thinking
of have too many strings to their bow, and can turn their backs
too easily on a thing that fails, for it to be safe work trusting to
their whims: it is not their fault, they cannot help it, but they
have no chance of spending time enough over the arts to know
anything practical of them, and they must of necessity be in the
hands of those who spend their time in pushing fashion this way
and that for their own advantage.

Morris's major experiments with dyed and printed textiles
began at this time, a period when British textile manufacture itself
had been extensively mechanised. To trace this process is to measure the decline in standards against which Morris was fighting
hard.

By the 1750s, the use of copper plates had superseded printing
from wooden blocks. These copper plates could carry more detail
than the wooden blocks but were still hand operated. Cloth was
laid out on long tables and the plates were pressed down and
reinked between each impression. This was a time-consuming
process requiring much accuracy, especially when designs of
many colours were used. Indeed, it was reckoned that one printer
could only produce six pieces of twenty-eight yards in a day. By
the end of the eighteenth century however the copper plates had
been converted into rollers and an entire length of cotton could be
printed by a wholly mechanical process. The introduction of
steam power increased such production yet further, and by the
start of the nineteenth century a single machine could produce
500 pieces a day. Annual production soared to sixteen million
pieces a year, and the country was able to supply huge quantities
of cheaply printed cotton to her vast markets overseas.

Such developments fostered the attitudes analysed by one expert witness called before the Commons Select Committee on Arts
and Manufactures in 1836:

The great object with every English manufacturer is quantity;
with him, that is always the best article to manufacture of which
the largest supply is required; he prefers much a large supply at a
low rate to a small supply at a higher; and that even should the
present profit be less from the former than from the latter,
because, in the long run, the larger the demand, the steadier it is
sure to be.

This process of mechanisation had been greatly helped by advances in the chemistry of dyeing. Since at least the seventeenth
century, analysts had been working to develop the ancient and

Opposite: *A photograph of
William Morris taken in the
1870s.*

traditional resources of available dyes, and by the time of the Great Exhibition a wide range of aniline dyes had come onto the market. These were often cheaper and easier to use than the older dyes, they offered a range of new colours (bright and unnatural though some of these were) while they also had the advantage of drying quickly and so helping to speed up the process of colour printing.

More sophisticated patterns largely failed however to meet the requirements of two-dimensional design advocated by such men as Owen Jones and Morris himself. Here, once again, a premium was set on the illusionistic and the ostentatious, qualities of design which the detailing permitted by copper plates helped to foster. The 'art' fabrics of the 1880s show a superabundance which is frequently grotesque in its restless self-display.

In The Lesser Arts *Morris shows the inseparable nature of good art and true living as he conceived these.*

There is a great deal of sham work in the world, hurtful to the buyer, more hurtful to the seller, if he only knew it, most hurtful to the maker: how good a foundation it would be towards getting good Decorative Art, that is ornamental workmanship, if we craftsmen were to resolve to turn out nothing but excellent workmanship in all things, instead of having, as we too often have now, a very low average standard of work, which we often fall below.

As so often, in his desire to innovate and improve, Morris went back to the past. In 1868, he wrote to Thomas Clarkson of the Bannister Hall Print Works in Lanarkshire inquiring about old printing blocks. Designs from the early 1830s were found. As George Wardle recalled: 'the processes of printing the patterns were not yet forgotten though long since superseded . . . . After a few trials the best of these patterns were reproduced in the original colourings and they took their place as novelties when exhibited in "the shop".' These patterns such as *Small Stem* had a white ground and clearly reflected eighteenth century tastes for the Chinese. They were printed, however, with synthetic dyes.

To advance beyond this point and create some of the most satisfying dyed and printed textiles of the period, Morris realised he would have to research into ancient traditions of dye manufacture. Modern aniline dyes could not finally satisfy him. While the deeper tones might be able to 'give up something to light and air and still have something left for the purchaser,' satisfactory results were difficult to obtain. 'Anyone wanting to produce dyed textiles with any artistic quality in them,' Morris eventually declared, 'must entirely forego the modern and commercial methods in favour of those which are at least as old as Pliny, who speaks of them as being old in his time.'

Morris believed it was necessary to return to a natural and often vegetable palate: indigo blues, red madder, weld yellow, the dyes obtained from barks, husks, roots and insect dyes such as red kermes. Initial experiments in Queen Square proved frustrating, and on George Wardle's suggestion Morris approached Wardle's brother Thomas, an independent dyer in Leek, Staffordshire, who was 'full of interest in the revived methods which he vaguely remembered as going on in his own boyhood and which some of his older workmen had practised'.

By February 1875, Morris had arrived at Leek and was experimenting with one of the most difficult of all dyes: indigo. Morris's hands turned blue with what he called this 'delightful work; hard for the body and easy to the mind'. Despite inevitable outbursts of exasperation, he eventually became expert in the three days preparation required for the hot vat, in the problems of oxidation and the qualities of smell—somewhat resembling 'that of stinking roast meat'—which indicated that the dye was ready.

I am dyeing yellows and reds: the yellows are very easy to get, and so are a lot of shades of salmon and flesh-colour & buff & orange: my chief difficulty is in getting a deep blood-red, but I hope to succeed before I come away: I have not got the proper indigo-vat for wool but I can dye blues in the cotton-vat and get lovely greens with that and the bright yellow that weld gives. This morning I assisted at the dyeing of 20 lbs of silk (for our damask) in the blue-vat; it was very exciting, as the thing is quite unused now, and we ran a good chance of spoiling the silk. There were 4 dyers & Mr Wardle at work, and myself as dyer's mate: the men were encouraged with beer & to it they went, and very pretty it was to see the silk coming green out of the vat & gradually turning blue. . . .

Morris's letter to his friend Mrs Coronio suggests the intense enthusiasm with which Morris worked at the mastering of new techniques.

Books on dyeing techniques were also exchanged between Morris and Wardle. Trial samples or 'fents' went backwards and forwards, often accompanied by tart letters from Morris on the shortcomings revealed by the tests the fents were exposed to. Colours were, he considered, too often 'dead and worked out' or 'too bright and crude.' Morris, thinking of the basis on which he ran his own Firm, was convinced that these problems stemmed from the inadequate supervision of Wardle's printer.

Eventually the man was replaced, and the experiments began to succeed more regularly. There is much in the correspondence between Morris and Wardle that shows how Morris, while prepared to invest generously in his research and development, could drive a hard bargain and even bully if he thought it necessary to getting his way. Nor was he necessarily averse to using modern chemicals and cutting labour costs provided that the appearance of the end product was not compromised.

For his early printed textiles, Morris returned to the old traditions of surface wooden block printing. These blocks were cut for him by craftsmen outside the Firm but always under his close supervision. This was a complex and intricate process. Tracings had first to be made from Morris's designs, each tracing corresponding to one colour in the original. These tracings were then checked by Morris for their accuracy before being transferred to the pearwood blocks which would then print each colour. Such a process could be an expensive business, especially with an ambitious design such as the excellent *Honeysuckle* of 1876. Various cloths could be printed with the blocks however and the *Honeysuckle* design was printed on linen, cotton, silk and other fabrics.

Right: *The printing block for Morris's design* Tulip. *Morris supervised the cutting of such blocks as these with exceptional care and many of them were often needed to produce one design.*

To print such designs, the material was first stretched on a blanket on one of the long printing tables. The block was then dipped in a dyepad, placed in position, usually with the help of pin-pricks of colour indicated on the selvedge, and struck with a 'mall' or lead weighted mallet. The print lengths were afterwards soaped and washed to clear the whites and test the fastness of the colours. They were then left to dry, preferably out of doors.

This method of manufacture was again a lengthy process since its various elements were often repeated. The cloths were passed through two soap and bran tubs, for example, washed and then dried for anything up to a week. Afterwards they were soaped, bran-washed and dried again, soaped for a fourth time and finally dried for a further six days. This usually proved sufficient, though a fifth soaping was suggested if results were not perfect.

The earliest of Morris's designs printed by Wardle were clearly influenced by experiments in wallpaper printing. *Marigold* in particular shows the influence of this area of his activity. Indeed, *Marigold*, along with *Tulip* and *Larkspur*, were used for both products. By the end of 1875, Morris's designs show the influence of the Indian printed fabrics which were being heavily

Below: *Morris's* Tulip *chintz of c. 1875 shows the great subtlety he had now achieved in balancing a formal, repeat design with lush natural elements.*

imported at this time. Some of these, *Indian Diaper* and *Anemone*, for example, have the hot, dark colourings characteristic of these sources, along with a rather tight employment of the motifs.

Morris was also developing other design solutions including the 'mirror' repeat or juxtaposition of reversed images. *Acanthus* and *African Marigold* are early examples of this, but by far the most successful is the *Honeysuckle*. The technique of the mirror repeat clearly appealed to the pleasure Morris derived from large designs, which were both more restful and more sumptuous than those that were tightly ordered. *Honeysuckle*, in particular, is a beautifully executed design with its interplay of reversed opening and full-blown flowers, its graceful pattern of tendrils, some vividly twisted around the thicker stalks, and its dense yet unobtrusive ground. Here, indeed, is Morris at his best, combining formal elements with a sensuous response to nature that is deeply satisfying.

Morris was also continuing to experiment with technical processes. In particular, he was to perfect the printing of fabrics through what is known as the 'indigo discharge method'. This technique was to help inspire some of his best designs, but it was not achieved without considerable difficulty.

In particular, Morris was dissatisfied with the results achieved by his collaboration with Thomas Wardle. The problem of supervision was again raising its head, and customers were returning defective samples. 'Tom Wardle is a heap of trouble to us,' Morris wrote in February 1881, 'nothing will he do right and he does write the longest winded letters containing lies of various kinds ... we shall have to take the chintzes ourselves before long and are now really looking for premises.'

By the middle of 1881, Morris had found these and moved into his Merton Abbey Works. Situated in a seven acre rural site watered by the River Wandle, which proved ideal for washing fabrics, Morris once again began experimenting with textile printing techniques.

The indigo discharge method can be seen particularly clearly in the *Wandle* design of 1884, so named 'to honour the helpful stream'. The basic blue of the fabric was achieved by soaking it in the indigo vat and leaving it to oxidize in the air. White or lighter blue areas of the design were then achieved by block-printing with a bleach that was partially diluted. The cloth was then washed, half dried, warmed and blockprinted with a 'mordant' to isolate those areas that were to receive the next colour. The cloth was then dipped in the appropriate vat. This process was repeated until all the required colourings appeared on the completed length. This technique (often enhanced by block printing) inspired some of Morris's finest designs, including the famous

Below: *The* Wandle *fabric of 1884 also shows Morris's use of the 'indigo discharge' method of dyeing.*

Strawberry Thief of 1883 which has always been one of his most popular patterns.

Just as a number of Morris's designs from the middle years of the 1870s were used for both fabric and wallpaper, so between 1882 and 1885 a further series of printed fabrics were also re-employed as wallpapers. While a few independent wallpaper designs from this period such as the light and graceful *Honeysuckle* of 1883 look back to the naturalism of the previous decade,

Above: *The* Honeysuckle *fabric of 1883.*

many of these combined wallpaper and fabric designs were influenced by Morris's historical researches in the textile collections of the Victoria and Albert, then known as the South Kensington Museum.

In The Lesser Arts *Morris demonstrates to his audience the necessary connection between the true artist and the ideals of social reform.*

If you can really fill your minds with memories of great works of art, and great times of art, you will, I think, be able to a certain extent to look through the aforesaid ugly surroundings, and will be moved to discontent of what is careless and brutal now, and will, I hope, at last be so much discontented with what is bad, that you will determine to bear no longer that shortsighted, reckless brutality of squalor that so disgraces our intricate civilisation.

'Perhaps I have used it as much as any man living,' Morris stated of this incomparable collection when giving evidence to the Royal Commission on Technical Instruction in 1882. Nonetheless, he was aware of the dangers as well as the benefits provided by such immense resources. 'However original a man may be,' he told the Commissioners, 'he cannot afford to disregard the works of art that have been produced in times past when design was flourishing; he is bound to study old examples, but he is also bound to supplement that by a careful study of nature, because if he does not he will certainly fall into a sort of cut and dried conventional method of designing . . . it takes a man of considerable originality to deal with old examples and to get what is good out of them without a making a design which lays itself open distinctly to the charge of plagiarism.'

A particularly good example of the independent use of the past, of tradition and nature, is the series of wallpapers and chintzes Morris named after English rivers, especially the tributaries of the Thames. This river had a particular significance for him, for it joined both symbolically and actually the two poles of his existence: Kelmscott Manor in Oxfordshire with its ideal world of nature, and Kelmscott House, the flat-fronted building on the Thames at Hammersmith where Morris had now moved his London residence. Mackail records that it was a great consolation to Morris '. . . to think that the waters that ran under his windows at Hammersmith had passed the meadows and gray gables of Kelmscott'. In the summer of 1880 and again in the following year, Morris's family and friends made their great river voyages between the two houses. Something of Morris's delight in these expeditions is revealed in *News from Nowhere* (1891) when, with the coming of a utopian new world, he imagines himself making a similar voyage and compares his delight in nature to the divided feelings he experienced in earlier and more polluted days:

> As we went higher up the river, there was less difference between the Thames of that day and the Thames as I remembered it; for setting aside the hideous vulgarity of the cockney villas of the well-to-do, stockbrokers and other such . . . this beginning of the country Thames was always beautiful; and as we slipped between the lovely greenery, I almost felt my youth come back to me, and as if I were on one of those water excursions which I used to enjoy so much in days when I was too happy to think there could be much amiss anywhere.

This feeling of life and summer greenery, of what was then felt to be nature's infinite power of self-renewal, is beautifully evoked by a design such as *Evenlode*. Its formal qualities of long and sinuous diagonals, decorated with flowers and leaves whose repetition across the width of the print gives the design its horizontal pattern, derive from an Italian cut velvet of the seventeenth century in the Victoria and Albert museum. Formal motifs have here been borrowed from the past and reinterpreted in the light of a powerful response to nature and an equally masterly sense of colour and design. 'Follow nature,' Morris was to tell his students, 'study antiquity, make your own art.'

Here Morris has fulfilled these aims, aims which are loose with the freedom of a man who pursues a particular craft rather than tight with the rigour of an academic who follows a different course. There is a joyous, aspiring quality about the *Evenlode* design, and to live for any length of time with the wallpapers and textiles of this period—the series named after rivers or the more stately *Bird and Anemone*—is continually to be sustained by their qualities of richness and their use of the natural qualities of the medium, their intellectual power and imaginative vision. As Morris himself declared:

> You may be as intricate and elaborate in your pattern as you please; nay, the more and more mysteriously you interweave your sprays and stems the better for your purpose, as the whole thing has to be pasted flat on a wall, and the cost of all this intricacy will but come out of your brain and hand. For the rest, the fact that we are in this art so little helped by beautiful and varying material imposes on us the necessity of being especially thoughtful in our designs; every one of them must have a distinct idea in it; some beautiful piece of nature must have pressed itself on our notice so forcibly that we are quite full of it, and can, by submitting ourselves to the rules of art, express our pleasure to

Above: *The* Evenlode *fabric of c. 1883 is one of those named after English rivers. It shows Morris's mature design at its best. The sinuous rhythms of the dominant motif are subtly counterpointed to the smaller tendrils whose tighter curves serve to lead the eye in a horizontal direction.*

Opposite: *The* Bird and Anemone *design of c. 1881 has a subdued but magisterial richness. It was used for both wallpaper and fabrics.*

others and give them some of the keen delight that we ourselves have felt.

The colours of Morris's mature designs, rich but unassertive, are a constant token of the better things of life, of a discrimination that seeks the truth rather than novelty. The patterns too are an endless source of delight. The individual motifs, flower and tendril and bird, realise exactly the fullness and mastery of their maker's mind. No detail is squashed or vague or strident. 'Remember,' Morris declared, 'that a pattern is either right or wrong. It cannot be forgiven for blundering. . . . It is with a pattern as with a fortress, it is no stronger than its weakest point. A failure forever recurring torments the eye too much to allow the mind to take any pleasure in suggestion and intention.'

There is also a balance between the formal and the naturalistic in these designs which is achieved quite without the irksome self-regard of the merely virtuoso. Here is an individual response to the ordering of nature which is clearly the vision of one man but which is something that is immediately felt to be common to all. The eye is neither bored by reading the design too easily nor stupefied with confusion as it admits the problem is beyond it. As Morris wrote in 1879:

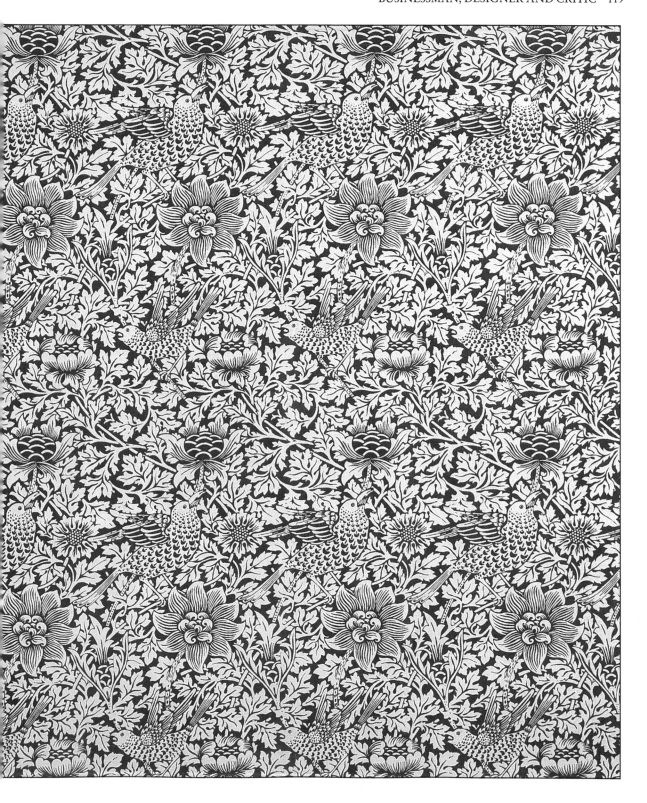

In all patterns that are meant to fill the eye and satisfy the mind, there should be a certain mystery. We should not be able to reach the whole thing at once, nor desire to do so, nor be compelled by that desire to go on tracing line after line to find out how the pattern is made, and I think the obvious presence of the geometrical order, if it be, as it should be, beautiful, tends towards this end, and prevents our feeling restless over a pattern.

In the papers and fabrics of this period, sinuous diagonals are perceived with that sense of joy which comes from ordering, but we do not feel we have been marshalled into a militaristic display. One clear direction is absorbed into another and perhaps richer motif until we are beguiled by yet further qualities, the rows of birds perhaps, or the abstract but sensuous weight of the opening flower heads.

These pleasures of variety are the pleasures of nature, while the satisfactions of order are those that a man derives from the harmonious mastery of his universe. In the end, we come to see the philosophic rightness of the design, that it is an interpretation of the world and of our place within it which is as valid and enriching as a great theory or piece of music: something life-enhancing rather than merely descriptive and which each time we turn to it gives us a freshness of response we might never have been able to invent but which seems always to have been known. To dismiss such activity merely as pattern-making, merely as 'wallpaper', is to dismiss those essential human qualities of interpreting the world and dignifying our mental and physical environments with what we can make of our best intuitions. Morris himself, who knew that bad design is like a moral slur, may have the last word on this: 'If we really care about art we shall not put up with something or other, but shall choose honest whitewash instead, on which sun and shadow play so pleasantly, if only our room be well planned and well shaped, and look kindly on us.'

Nature as the basis of good art and good art as the basis of a moral society is a constant theme in Morris's lectures.

For, and this is at the root of the whole matter, everything made by man's hands has a form, which must be either beautiful or ugly; beautiful if it is in accord with Nature, and helps her; ugly if it is discordant with Nature, and thwarts her; it cannot be indifferent: we, for our parts, are busy or sluggish, eager or unhappy, and our eyes are apt to get dulled to this eventfulness of form in those things which we are always looking at. Now it is one of the chief uses of decoration, the chief part of its alliance with nature, that it has to sharpen our dulled senses in this matter: for this end are those wonders of intricate patterns interwoven, those strange forms invented, which men have so long delighted in: forms and intricacies that do not necessarily imitate nature, but in which the hand of the craftsman is guided to work in the way that she does, till the web, the cup, or the knife, look as natural, nay as lovely, as the green field, the river bank, or the mountain flint.

To give people pleasure in the things they must perforce *use*, that is one great office of decoration; to give people pleasure in the things they must perforce *make*, that is the other use of it.

Sustained by such ideas, and working with his familiar prodigious energy, Morris was also showing a keen interest in woven materials. These show his delight in texture, colour and richness of effect.

To realise these, Morris was perfectly content to use power-driven jacquard looms employed in the factories that wove his firm's designs, provided they produced textiles of high quality. Discussing weaving, Morris declared: 'since the manner of doing it has with some few exceptions varied little for many hundred years, such trivial alterations as the lifting of the warp threads by means of the jacquard machine, or throwing the shuttles by steam power, ought not to make much difference in the art of it.' Morris was not an inveterate enemy of the machine. What he objected to was its being exploited for profit over quality and so degrading the work of the labourer.

As so often, however, there were problems of both quality and delivery in the use of sub-contracted manufacturers, and by 1877 Morris was being 'dazzled' by the prospect of weaving his own textiles. As always, he was determined thoroughly to familiarise himself with the techniques of production, and to achieve this he hired a weaver from France and moved him and his loom into Queen Square.

After initial delays, such sumptuous fabrics as *Anemone* were being woven. Some of the most exciting of these fabrics, *Bird*, for example, show Morris's use of animal motifs at this time, while *Peacock and Dragon* shows his original use of items in the Victoria and Albert Museum. He was particularly influenced by a fourteenth century Italian textile which was, he declared: 'designed in the heyday of medieval art, uniting the wild fantasy and luxurious intricacy of the East, with the straight-forward story-telling imagination and clear definite drawing of medieval Europe.' Under the influence of Middle and Far Eastern patterns, also seen in the Victoria and Albert Museum, Morris created such exotic pieces as *Brocatel* and *Isphahan*. These reflect his growing awareness of oriental colour.

Right: *A fourteenth century Sicilian textile from the Victoria and Albert Museum. This is an example of the medieval fabric design that was to have so great an influence on Morris's work.*

Great richness of effect was also gained by weaving double cloths of silk and wool. The result has a beautiful variation of texture and sheen and was especially suited to curtains where the play of light over the folds is particularly satisfying. Such silk and wool double cloths as *Dove and Rose* could be woven in five colours and in one example was brocaded with gold thread. This pursuit of luxurious effects can also be seen in *St James*, a commission received from the Palace in 1881. Here, flower and leaf forms curl in lively silhouette over the various lights of figured and damasked silk. Textiles such as these were, of course, exceptionally expensive. Morris quoted £245 for a set of *St James* curtains, but their remarkable quality has given them a long life.

Morris's interest in textile manufacture included designs for the carpets that were often so essential a part of his interior decoration schemes. He designed carpets for both machine manufacture as well as the hand-knotted or 'Hammersmith' carpets which should be considered as separate works in their own right.

Above: *Morris's* Peacock and Dragon *design of 1878 is one of his more sumptuous and is clearly influenced by the oriental and medieval fabrics he was studying in the Victoria and Albert Museum.*

Though Morris regarded machine made carpets as 'make-shifts for cheapness' sake,' he experimented with a wide variety of machine techniques: Kidderminster carpets with small motifs such as *Daisy* which proved to be very popular and useable, various types of Axminster carpet, and, above all, Brussels cord and Wilton pile carpets.

Brussels cord was a hard-wearing loop carpet with two weft threads in each row of pile. In the Wilton piles, three weft threads were used and the loops were cut to produce a soft texture. Of these last, the Firm's brochure for the 1883 Boston Fair declared: 'Wiltons must be classed as the best kind of machine woven carpets . . . if well made the material is very durable, and by skilful treatment in the designing, the restrictions as to colour are not noticeable.'

In designs such as *Lily*, *Bellflowers* and *Rose*, which Morris created between 1875 and '76, these restrictions were used to great creative effect. Simplicity of motif had been achieved as well as a progressive softening of the overall effect. The somewhat cramped and fussy design of *Lily*, for example, is broadened into stronger motifs in *Bellflowers*, while in *Rose* an extremely successful combination of colour, texture and motif results in a design which is both quiet and sumptuous, appealing to the touch and the eye as well as to the pleasures of formal ornament. *Rose* is the work of a man whose feelings for the fundamental qualities of carpet design was deep and intuitive as well as being based on wide experience.

Indeed, Morris was now regarded as the foremost English expert on Persian and Turkish carpets, and in this capacity he was appointed in 1883 as an Art Referee to guide the Victoria and Albert museum in its acquisitions. It was on Morris's recommendation (and partly with his financial help) that the museum eventually acquired the magnificent *Ardabil* carpet, still one of its greatest possessions.

Morris's stated aim in his own production was '. . . to make England independent of the East for carpets that may claim to be considered as works of art'. He deplored the low quality of the work currently being imported with its evident signs of the bastardisation of native values through the pressures of British commercialism.

As early as 1877 he had begun experimenting with small, Chinese inspired designs intended to be hung on walls. In these pieces he rejected utterly any attempt at three dimensional illusion, just as he was opposed to the purely geometric. 'I, as a Western man and picture lover,' he later declared, 'must still insist on plenty of meaning in your patterns. I must have unmistakable suggestions of gardens and fields and strange trees, boughs and tendrils or I can't do with your patterns.'

In The Art of the People *Morris manifests his utter contempt for the effects of English imperialism on native conquered peoples.*

I daresay many of you will remember how emphatically those who first had to do with the movement of which the foundation of our art-schools was a part, called the attention of our pattern-designers to the beautiful works of the East. This was surely most well judged of them, for they bade us look at an art at once beautiful, orderly, living in our own day, and above all, popular. Now, it is a grievous result of the sickness of civilisation that this art is fast disappearing before the advance of western conquest and commerce—fast, and every day faster. While we are met here in Birmingham to further the spread of education in art,

Englishmen in India are, in their short-sightedness, actively destroying the very sources of that education—jewellery, metal-work, pottery, calico-printing, brocade-weaving, carpet-making—all the famous and historical arts of the great peninsula have been for long treated as matters of no importance, to be thrust aside for the advantage of any paltry scrap of so-called commerce; and matters are now speedily coming to an end there.

By 1879, the outbuildings at Kelmscott House had been converted into weaving sheds and Morris now began to produce the larger 'Hammersmith' rugs. These again show a Chinese influence, though the great design advance made here is the possibility of reading these patterns from any direction. It was the move to the greater spaciousness of Merton Abbey however that freed Morris to produce his first large-scale carpet designs.

At Merton Abbey, young girls sat on low benches in front of looms anything up to twenty-five feet in length. With the design on point-paper and with the magnificently dyed yarns cut into two inch tufts, they built up rows of Turkish knots, beating these down when each row was completed until a density of something like twenty-eight knots to the inch was achieved.

The earliest of Morris's large carpet commissions have either been lost or have to be reconstructed from photographs and drawings. The first carpet woven for George Howard, for example, has completely disappeared. The enormous arc-shaped carpet woven for Lord Portsmouth had a red border while the

Above: The rioting vulgarity of this carpet by H. Brinton of Kidderminster suggests the false values of design Morris was to strive against in his own work as a carpet maker.

indigo ground was decorated with armorial bearings and mottos interspersed with foliage. This colour-scheme was often adopted by Morris—it was an exceptionally rich combination—and may have have been used on the carpets woven for Sir Isaac Lothian Bell's home at Rounton Grange. Here, the ground of the carpet was decorated with dense patterns of willow and acanthus leaves curling round flowers and buds.

Carpets such as the *Swan House* of 1881 have the somewhat mechanical effect of quartered mirror designs and resemble Persian examples. Undoubtedly the finest of these early large carpets was that woven for Alexander Ionides in 1883 at the cost of £113. This, indeed, was an exceptional work, and is all the more remarkable when it is remembered that its qualities of colour and design were achieved by Morris quite independently of any long established national tradition of such production. Its colours are beautifully rich and subtle, while its design is no slavish imitation of its models. The light blue tendrils have something of the satisfying, flat and abstract naturalism of the best medieval iron door

Below: *Three versions of the magnificent* Holland Park *carpet of 1883 were woven, and the design is Morris's most successful synthesis of Medieval and Eastern motifs.*

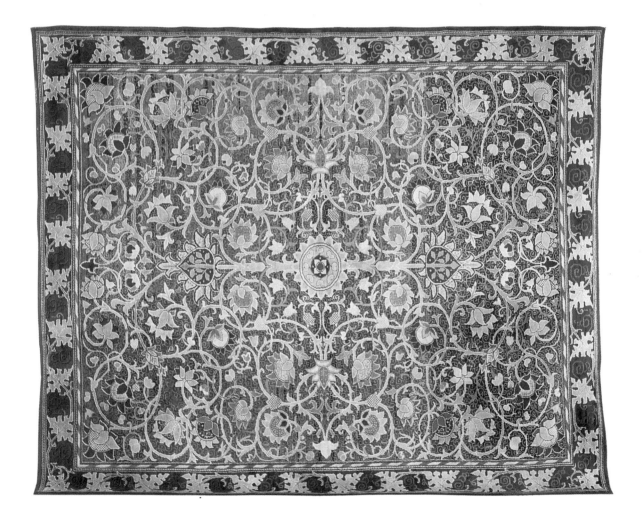

furniture and frescoed foliage. The flowerheads have a character-istic opulent variety, while the competence of the whole points forward to the great achievements of the late 1880s and '90s.

A number of Morris's richer clients shared his enthusiasm for tapestry. In a sharp rejection of the woven imitation of oil paint-ings then practised by the Gobelins factory, Morris turned back to the great work of the medieval Flemish weavers. In 1877, he set up a tapestry loom in his bedroom at Kelmscott House, choosing the *haute lisse* or upright loom in which the back of the tapestry faces the weaver while the front is seen reflected in a mirror. By 1879, and after over five hundred hours of work, Morris pro-duced his first tapestry. This, properly known as *Acanthus and Vine* but soon nicknamed *Cabbage and Vine* because of its great openly curling leaves, is a *verdure* or design of plant and animal forms in a basic blue and green colouring. It is a piece of some quality and a notable experiment, but the most fruitful period of the Firm's tapestries was still to come.

Below: *This magnificent verdure was Morris's first tapestry and was woven by him at Kelmscott House in 516 hours during 1879. Properly called* Acanthus and Vine, *it was nicknamed 'Cabbage and Vine' because of the undisciplined curling of the leaves.*

Embroidery design and manufacture were also proceeding apace, and the Firm now employed a number of professional needlewomen. Here Morris's daughter May played an important role in both administration and design. This was some relief to Morris, since these highly skilled artisans could be 'bothering' about money, and a distinct note of exasperation crept into Morris's letters when he complained how 'The embroidery ladies gave me such a turn this morning. I thought I should have been walked and talked off my legs.' With the mutual respect of true craftsmen however, Morris was also quick to appreciate and learn from the skills of such able practitioners as Mrs Catherine Holiday with whom he produced some of his most distinctive designs. These include the admirable pattern of sunflowers on indigo blue linen embroidered for the Earl of Southampton.

While the Firm employed needlewomen and hired outworkers they also produced designs for the leisured wives of wealthy clients. Hangings of typically stylised fruit and flowers produced for these women reveal Morris's study of the antique Eastern and Italian textiles in the Victoria and Albert Museum. In all cases the stitches in these pieces serve to accentuate the linearity of the design rather than being an end in themselves.

Many of Morris's wealthy embroiderers such as Margaret Beale of Standen, East Sussex were also exceptionally able practitioners of their craft, as can be seen from the *Artichoke* hanging embroidered by Mrs Beale and her daughters from 1877. Indeed, the designs such women embroidered were often large and essential elements in the decorative schemes Morris designed for their houses. This is particularly clear with the hangings based on *The Romance of the Rose* and embroidered in wool, silk and gold thread by Lady Bell and her daughters for the dining room at Rounton Grange. Here, as with the many designs also prepared for the Royal School of Art Needlework, the figures were by Burne-Jones while the complex decorative backgrounds were by Morris.

The schemes of interior decoration in which these luxurious creations were used derive from the original designs for the Red House. Though towards the end of his career Morris's interiors were to become lighter and less cluttered, his rooms of the 1880's were still somewhat sombre and crowded.

Ceilings and panelling were sometimes painted white, though more lavish schemes employed patterned ceiling papers or gilded and painted coffering. Walls, when they were not covered by embroideries and tapestries, were also painted, papered or hung with silk. There were often rugs on the floors to offset the gleam of polished boards. Chairs were upholstered, frequently in the same design as the curtains, while where fireplaces were canopied and tiled, their shelves displayed collections of Defltware or de

Morgan pots. Reds and yellows provided a feeling of warmth, while cabinets often displayed clients' more valuable items such as the bronzes and Tanagra figures of Alexander Ionides in his house at Holland Park.

Indeed, photographs allow us to see the very considerable luxury in which this Greek merchant lived. The magnificent panelled staircase, for example, was laid with a machine made Axminster on cinnamon and blue. The Antiquities Room, rich and crowded, had Morris fabrics and embroideries and a Morris carpet. Chandeliers hung from the papered ceilings. In the study, *Forest* tapestries hung on the walls and there were Morris fabrics on the chairs and tables. The entire scheme took eight years to complete and cost well over £2000, Morris's visits for consultation being charged at about £2 10 s each.

Larger though less crowded schemes were also arranged for Rounton Grange, now, alas, demolished. Yet it was here, in 1876, that a small incident occurred which provides a vivid insight into Morris's thought at this time. The owner of Rounton Grange, Sir Isaac Lothian Bell, heard Morris walking about excitedly and talking to himself. Bell went over to him and asked what was the matter. 'He turned on me like a wild animal,' Bell later recalled, and he burst out: 'It's only that I spend my life in ministering to the swinish luxury of the rich!'

Morris's anger is the more telling for its bitter self-reproach, but although his resentment here spilled out in an unguarded moment, it is full of that critical energy he was soon to express more coherently in his lectures. These, begun in 1877, were first collected five years later and published under the title *Hopes and Fears for Art*.

The lectures show how far Morris's thought had developed from the 'art for art's sake stance' of his early poetry. In their strong and sometimes caustic prose, these lectures reveal a man altogether more seriously committed to the social problems of real life in the Earthly Paradise. Dreams of escape are no longer enough. Morris realised he must now face the squalor and inequality of Victorian industrial society full on. In returning to develop the ideas of his first teacher John Ruskin, he was also unconsciously feeling his way towards the work of his final master, Karl Marx. *Hopes and Fears for Art* is thus a central work in his development.

At the core of Morris's concern lies that central Ruskinian theme: anger at the corroding effect of mindless commercialism. Once again it is shown that industrial man, in his concern with profits alone, has degraded taste and polluted the natural world. In setting up his horrific factories, he has divorced mankind from the true spiritual satisfactions of work and forced his fellows into the enmity of class warfare, of rich against poor and poor against

Right: *This linen coverlet was embroidered by Mrs Catherine Holiday from a Morris design of c. 1876. It suggests not only the quality of Morris's mature work but the immense skill of the lady amateurs who worked his patterns.*

rich. Man has been sundered from beauty, from nature and his own kind. Completeness of life has been denied him and his spirit has been crushed. Work, which should be his fulfilment, is now merely labour, toiling for the bitter bread of poverty.

Morris's love for the English countryside was a profound influence on his work.

. . . but when we can get beyond that smoky world, there, out in the country we may still see the works of our fathers yet alive amidst the very nature they were wrought into, and of which they are so completely a part: for there indeed if anywhere, in the English country, in the days when people cared about such things, was there a full sympathy between the works of man and the land they were made for. . . .

The true work in which men should seek their salvation is the work of the artist and the craftsman, what Morris, following Ruskin, called 'the expression by man of his pleasure in labour'. This has nothing to do with the horrors of exploitation and greed, with bitter, soulless people producing unnatural and vulgar objects that no one can really want. Instead of conspicuous waste, there should be community and joy. Eventually, men will learn to make things honestly and beautifully for each other. Their motive will not be profit but human fulfilment. The result will be true art 'made by the people and for the people, as a happiness to the maker and user'. Vulgar luxury and the slavery of the factory will disappear when men regain natural simplicity of taste and learn once more to follow the golden rule: '*Have nothing in your houses that you do not know to be useful, or believe to be beautiful.*'

Morris's most famous statement of his beliefs occurs in this passage from his lecture The Beauty of Life.

Believe me, if we want art to begin at home, as it must, we must clear our houses of troublesome superfluities that are for ever in our way: conventional comforts that are no real comforts, and do but make work for servants and doctors: if you want a golden rule that will fit everybody, this is it:

'*Have nothing in your houses that you do not know to be useful, or believe to be beautiful.*'

And if we apply that rule strictly, we shall in the first place show the builders and such-like servants of the public what we really want, we shall create a demand for real art, as the phrase goes; and in the second place, we shall surely have more money to pay for decent houses.

As greed of unfair gain, wanting to be paid for what we have not earned, cumbers our path with this tangle of bad work, of sham work, so that heaped-up money which this greed has brought us (for greed will have its way, like all other strong passions), this money, I say, gathered into heaps little and big, with all the false distinction which so unhappily it yet commands amongst us, has raised up against the arts a barrier of the love of luxury and show, which is of all obvious hindrances the worst to overpass: the highest and most cultivated classes are not free from the vulgarity of it, the lower are not free from its pretence. I beg you to remember both as a remedy against this, and as explaining exactly what I mean, that nothing can be a work of art which is not useful; that is to say, which does not minister to the body when well under command of the mind, or which does not amuse, soothe, or elevate the mind in a healthy state. What tons upon tons of unutterable rubbish pretending to be works of art in some degree would this maxim clear out of our London houses, if it were understood and acted upon! To my mind it is only here and there (out of the kitchen) that you can find in a well-to-do house things that are of any use at all: as a rule all the decoration (so called) that has got there is there for the sake of show, not because anybody likes it.

Morris saw clearly that an industrial society producing superfluous and ugly artefacts was an appalling waste of human initiative.

It was such virtuous simplicity which, Morris believed, accounted for the great achievements of medieval art. Like Ruskin, he considered the medieval craftsman to be just such an ordinary man as we should all ideally become, effortlessly producing the finest artifacts in the course of daily labour. For the medieval workman, it seemed, there was no division between art and craft or between man and his environment.

That thing which I understand by real art is the expression by man of his pleasure in labour. I do not believe he can be happy in his labour without expressing that happiness; and especially is this so when he is at work at anything in which he specially excels.

In The Lesser Arts *Morris portrayed his ideal of art arising from a natural and healthy society.*

Hence the supreme importance of returning to a study of the past in order to understand the original dignity that man might yet re-attain. In 'The Lesser Arts', a lecture first given in 1877, such notions rise to a paean in praise of all that Morris held most dear. The countryside of southern England, mild yet variegated with the constant interchange of natural beauty, is rightly seen as rich in historical associations and centuries of reverence. Care, sympathy, homeliness and even the commonplace become tokens of moral and emotional truths. There is nothing here, it is alleged, that speaks of tyranny and ostentation. Rather, a 'peasant art' produced a uniquely English beauty, the art of ordinary people living in harmony with nature, unstrained and intuitively moral.

Morris's belief in a medieval art of the people was fundamental to his thinking.

For as was the land, such was the art of it while folk yet troubled themselves about such things; it strove little to impress people either by pomp or ingenuity: not unseldom it fell into commonplace, rarely it rose into majesty; yet was it never oppressive, never a slave's nightmare nor an insolent boast: and at its best it had an inventiveness, an individuality that grander styles have never overpassed: its best too, and that was in its very heart, was given as freely to the yeoman's house, and the humble village church, as to the lord's palace or the mighty cathedral: never coarse, though often rude enough, sweet, natural and unaffected, an art of peasants rather than of merchant-princes or courtiers, it must be a hard heart, I think, that does not love it: whether a man has been born among it like ourselves, or has come wonderingly on its simplicity from all the grandeur overseas.

Gothic architecture is the chief glory of this, and Gothic cathedrals the jewels in its crown. Salisbury cathedral in particular reveals '. . . a complete and logical style with no longer anything to apologise for, claiming homage from the intellect, as well as the imagination of man.' The great building is organic, human and true. It is, Morris declares, sweet yet lofty. It fulfils the highest purpose of art which is '. . . the expression of reverence for nature, and the crown of nature, the life of man upon the earth.'

Such buildings were nonetheless in terrible danger. The enthusiastic vulgarity of the age was spoiling even these monuments as architects like Gilbert Scott, inspired by the Cambridge Camden Society, set about their baleful work of 'restoration'. The restorers were impelled by a spurious ideal of uniformity. Nothing it was believed should confuse what could be guessed of the original architects' intentions. But the slow growth of even the humblest church—the addition of an Early English nave to a Norman porch, a Decorated window casting its light on a Georgian tomb—provided a continuity to which Morris could respond with something approaching physical satisfaction.

But of late years a great uprising of ecclesiastical zeal, coinciding with a great increase of study, and consequently of knowledge of mediæval architecture, has driven people into spending their money on these buildings, not merely with the purpose of repairing them, of keeping them safe, clean, and wind- and water-tight, but also of 'restoring' them to some ideal state of perfection; sweeping away if possible all signs of what has befallen them at least since the Reformation, and often since dates much earlier. . . .

This passage shows the feelings that were to lead Morris to found the Society for the Preservation of Ancient Buildings.

Fashion nonetheless dictated other ideals and, for a long time, Morris followed fashion. In 1853, for example, the year Morris went up to Oxford, Sir George Gilbert Scott had torn out the fourteenth century window of Christ Church cathedral and replaced it with a 'Norman' version of his own devising. Morris himself had later helped in such 'restorations' at three Cambridge colleges and had provided stained glass for a large number of ancient churches. Now, as he started to question the values of his society more acutely, he came to see that such improvements could be counted as no more than high-minded vandalism, an evil perpetrated against an inheritance which a barbarous age could not appreciate. In 1876, he was horrified to see the damage being done to the parish church at Burford near Kelmscott. The following year he read of Scott's proposal to 'restore' Tewkesbury Abbey. He wrote to *The Athenaeum* with a withering sarcasm born of new and passionate conviction:

Sir,
    My eye just now caught the word 'restoration' in the morning paper, and, on looking closer, I saw that this time it is nothing less than the minster of Tewkesbury that is to be destroyed by Sir Gilbert Scott. Is it altogether too late to do something to save it—and whatever else of beautiful or historical is still left us on the sites of the ancient buildings we were once so famous for? Would it not be of some use once and for all and with the least delay possible to set on foot an association for the purpose of watching over and protecting these relics, which, scanty as they

are now become, are still wonderful treasures, all the more priceless in this age of the world, when the newly-invented study of living history is the chief joy of so many of our lives?

He proposed a defence committee be formed immediately:

What I wish for therefore is that an association be set on foot to keep watch on old monuments, to protest against all 'restoration' that means more than keeping out wind and weather, and, by all means, literary and other, to awaken a feeling that our ancient buildings are not mere ecclesiastical toys but sacred monuments of the nation's growth and hope.

Morris acted swiftly. In March 1877, a meeting was held at 449 Oxford Street. Present were Carlyle, Ruskin, Burne-Jones, Philip Webb and Morris as secretary. It was a congregation of the greatest Victorian sages, and from their joint labours emerged the Society for the Protection of Ancient Buildings, familiarly known as 'Anti-Scrape'.

In the Society's manifesto, Morris proposed an ideal whose caring honesty is of abiding importance. Old buildings, he wrote 'are not in any sense our property, to do as we like with them. We are only trustees for those that come after us'. Numerous campaigns were fought under this banner. Westminster Abbey and Westminster Hall, the school buildings at Eton and the churches of London were all saved from the mania for 'restoration'. When it was proposed that the west front of St Mark's cathedral in Venice be tampered with, Gladstone and Disraeli, divided on almost everything else, lent their weight to the international protest. In 1882, the Ancient Monuments Protection Act was voted through Parliament and allowed for important old buildings to be taken into public ownership.

Morris's work for the 'Anti-Scrape' is one of his abiding legacies, yet his life in the 1870s and early 1880s was riddled with the most uncomfortable divisions. On the one hand he was at the pinnacle of a career many lesser men could have been justly proud of. The vast energy of his enthusiasms, his obsessive pursuit of excellence in design and manufacture, had raised many crafts to new heights and with such achievements came commercial success. At 449 Oxford Street, a wealthy clientele chose furniture, fabrics and wallpapers. In 1886, Morris was commissioned to design a paper of crowns and thistles to decorate Balmoral, the new Scottish residence of Queen Victoria.

As I sit at my work at home, which is at Hammersmith, close to the river, I often hear some of that ruffianism go past the window of which a good deal has been said in the papers of late, and has been said before at recurring periods. As I hear the yells and shrieks and all the degradation cast on the glorious tongue of Shakespeare and Milton, as I see the brutal reckless faces and figures go past me, it rouses the recklessness and brutality in me also, and fierce wrath takes possession of me, till I remember, as I hope I mostly do, that it was my good luck only of being born respectable and rich, that has put me on this side of the window among delightful books and lovely works of art, and not on the other side, in the empty street, the drink-steeped liquor-shops, the foul and degraded lodgings. I know by my own feelings and desires what these men want, what would have saved them from this lowest depth of savagery: employment which would foster their self-respect and win the praise and sympathy of their fellows, and dwellings which they could come to with pleasure, surroundings which would soothe and elevate them; reasonable labour, reasonable rest. There is only one thing that can give them this—art.

Morris's personal sympathy for the plight of the poor was deeply felt. He was also aware of what divided him from truly sharing their troubles.

Yet the pursuit of excellence had served to show ever more painfully the injustice and spiritual crippling of the modern worlds of commerce and industry. Morris remained acutely aware of something rotten at the very core of society. There were times when this realisation bordered on despair. 'If civilisation is to go no further than this,' he told an audience in 1880, 'it had better not have gone so far: if it does not aim at getting rid of this misery and giving some share in the happiness and dignity to *all* the people that it has created . . . it is simply an organised injustice, a mere instrument for oppression, so much the worse than that which has gone before it, as its pretensions are higher, its slavery subtler, its mastery harder to overthrow, because supported by such a dense mass of commonplace well being and comfort.'

Morris had sought to hide from this bitter knowledge in dreams and poetry, he had sought to counter it with his craft and sought to expose it in his lectures. Now, at the height of professional success, he was to make the most daring challenge of all and commit himself to political action in the attempt to improve his world.

Unjust War

Proof to
W. Morris, Esq
26 Queen Square
Bloomsbury

(1)

To the Working-men of England

Friends and fellow-citizens,

There is danger of war; bestir yourselves
to face that danger: if you go to sleep, saying, we do not
understand it, and the danger is far off, you may wake
and find the evil fallen upon you, for even now it is at the
door.   Take heed in time and consider it well, for a
hard matter it will be for most of us to bear war-taxes,
war-prices, war-losses of wealth and work, and friends and kindred:
We shall pay heavily, and you, friends of the Working-classes,
will pay the heaviest.

And what shall we buy at this heavy price? Will it be glory,
and wealth and peace for those that come after us?
Alas! no; for these are the aims of a just war; but
if we wage the unjust war that fools and cowards are bidding
us wage today, our loss of wealth will buy us fresh
loss of wealth, our loss of work will buy us loss of hope,
our loss of friends and kindred will buy us enemies
from father to son.

I say an unjust war: for do not be deceived! if
we go to war with Russia now, it will not be to punish
her for evil deeds done, or to hinder her from evil
deeds hereafter, but to put down just insurrection against
the thieves and murderers of Turkey; to stir up a
faint pleasure in the hearts of the do-nothing fools that cry out without
meaning for a 'spirited foreign policy'; to guard our
well-beloved rule in India from the coward fear of
an invasion that may happen a hundred years hence —
or never; to exhibit our army and navy once
more before the wondering eyes of Europe; to give a little hope

REVOLUTIONARY SOCIALIST

To enter Victorian politics was to confront an empire. It was to see at first hand the workings of British imperialism, the might of her industry and the full horror of the social inequalities forced on her people by the workings of capitalism. Here was an experience that was to absorb Morris's energies, channel his thoughts and eventually focus his hopes on an ideal of human perfection. The disillusioned Liberal became a radical Marxist. His confrontation with the age was complete.

Morris's active involvement with politics dates from 1876. In that year the English government under the premiership of Disraeli seemed ready to join the Turks and wage war against Russia. The underlying reason for this was commercial. Disraeli saw clearly that if the Russians invaded the Balkans and succeeded in freeing their 'Christian brothers', they would also control the Dardanelles and hence England's trade route with her Indian empire. Since India was the jewel in the imperial crown, it seemed to Disraeli that an alliance with the Turks overrode any moral objection to the atrocities the Turks themselves had recently committed on the Balkan peoples. To protect the imperial dream, Disraeli was prepared to ally his country with what Morris called 'a gang of thieves and murderers'.

His indignation boiled over in a letter to the Liberal *Daily News*, and, indeed, it was the Liberals of the parliamentary opposition, under the canny leadership of Gladstone, who were now organising rallies and demonstrations against Disraeli's policies. Feelings continued to run high, stoked by Disraeli himself and his patriotic war party who now had a song which was to add a new word to the English language:

We don't want to fight,
But, by Jingo, if we do,
We've got the ships, we've got the men,
We've got the money too!

Opposite: *The manuscript of Morris's first major political pamphlet* Unjust War *addressed 'To the Working Men of England'.*

Morris, who was revolted by such attitudes, wrote a rival version which was sung at meetings of the Eastern Question Association of which he was now Treasurer:

Wake, London lads, wake, bold and free!
   Arise and fall to work,
Lest England's glory come to be
   Bond servant to the Turk!

What these verses reveal, undistinguished though they might be, is Morris's realisation of the power that lay in the efficient organisation of the ordinary working people of the country, men such as Henry Broadhurst and George Howell of the Labour Representation League. By April of 1877, Morris had addressed his pamphlet *Unjust War* 'To the Working Men of England'. This was a clear attempt to portray the Balkan question in class terms. In particular, Morris urges the working people to see that those who oppress them in everyday life are those who would also lead them into an immoral struggle. With an anger and irony not seen in his prose before, Morris inveighs against stock brokers, press barons, the idle rich and the 'Tory Rump'. Here was a presage of things to come.

As the Liberal Party began to trim its sails, and moderate the appearance of idealism it had brought to the Balkan issue, so Morris gained a deepening respect for the firm stance taken by these working men, some of whom still did not have the vote. Experience was educating Morris in the virtues of a proletarian world he had barely known before, and this faith was to outlive his initial reaction to the ignominious conclusion of the Anti-Turk campaign and its revelations of Tory guile and Liberal opportunism: the conventional power-play of the professional parliamentarians. This Morris was to hold in increasing contempt. When the Gladstone government of 1880 failed to effect radical reform at home, coerced the Irish and marched into Egypt and Sudan, Morris's disillusion with Liberalism was complete.

This passage from Marx's Capital *shrewdly analyses the position Morris was to adopt.*

Finally, in times when the class struggle nears the decisive hour, the process of dissolution going on within the ruling class, in fact within the whole range of old society, assumes such a violent, glaring character, that a small section of the ruling class cuts itself adrift, and joins the revolutionary class, the class that holds the future in its hands. Just as, therefore, at an earlier period, a section of the nobility went over to the bourgeoisie, so now a portion of the bourgeoisie goes over to the proletariat, and in particular, a portion of the bourgeois ideologists, who have raised themselves to the level of comprehending theoretically the historical movement as a whole.

Nonetheless, as he watched Broadhurst and Howell rapidly becoming willing pawns of the Liberal party, so Morris also began to have an equal disregard for the most obvious focus of working class political activity: the Trades Unions. Though founded for the advancement of the working classes, Morris was to declare that they '. . . have already become conservative and obstructive bodies, wielded by the middle-class politicians for party purposes'. His concern over the crippling effects of social injustice ran too deep however for cynicism to triumph for long. As Morris was later to declare:

Below: *A photograph of Karl Marx.*

The consciousness of revolution stirring amidst our hateful modern society prevented me, luckier than many others of artistic perceptions, from crystallising into a mere railer against progress, on the one hand, and on the other from wasting time and energy in any of the nervous schemes by which the quasi-artistic of the middle classes hope to make art grow when it no longer has any root, and thus I became a practical Socialist.

By 1882, Morris felt himself ready '. . . to join any body who distinctly called themselves Socialists'. In January of the following year he became a part of The Social Democratic Foundation, signing his membership card 'William Morris, Designer'. A month later he was studying Marx in a French translation.

... what I mean by Socialism is a condition of society in which there should be neither rich nor poor, neither master nor master's man, neither idle nor overworked, neither brain-sick brain workers, nor heart-sick hand workers, in a word, in which all men would be living in equality of condition, and would manage their affairs unwastefully, and with the full consciousness that harm to one would mean harm to all—the realization at last of the meaning of the word COMMONWEALTH.

Morris lucidly summed up his political ideal in How I Became a Socialist. *This is an excellent short memoir in which he traces the origins of his political views with striking power.*

Apart from the desire to produce beautiful things, the leading passion of my life has been and is hatred of modern civilization. What shall I say of it now, when the words are put into my mouth, my hope of its destruction – what shall I say of its supplanting by Socialism?

Morris's conversion to socialism was based not only on Marxist theory but a profound and personal revulsion at the conditions of nineteenth century England.

What shall I say concerning its mastery of and its waste of mechanical power, its commonwealth so poor, its enemies of the commonwealth so rich, its stupendous organization – for the misery of life! Its contempt of simple pleasures which everyone could enjoy but for its folly? Its eyeless vulgarity which has destroyed art, the one certain solace of labour? All this I felt then as now, but I did not know why it was so. The hope of the past times was gone, the struggles of mankind for many ages had produced nothing but this sordid, aimless, ugly confusion; the immediate future seemed to me likely to intensify all the present evils by sweeping away the last survivals of the days before the dull squalor of civilization had settled down on the world. This was a bad look-out indeed, and, if I may mention myself as a personality and not as a mere type, especially so to a man of my disposition, careless of metaphysics and religion, as well as of scientific analysis, but with a deep love of the earth and the life on it, and a passion for the history of the past of mankind. Think of it! Was it all to end in a counting-house on the top of a cinder-heap, with Podsnap's drawing-room in the offing, and a Whig committee dealing out champagne to the rich and margarine to the poor in such convenient proportions as would make all men contented together, though the pleasure of the eyes was gone from the world, and the place of Homer was to be taken by Huxley?

From How I Became a Socialist.

To sum up, then, the study of history and the love and practice of art forced me into a hatred of the civilization which, if things were to stop as they are, would turn history into inconsequent nonsense, and make art a collection of the curiosities of the past, which would have no serious relation to the life of the present.

Since the decline of the Chartist movement in the 1840s, no radical group in England had been fired by the fundamental belief that democracy should be interpreted to mean rule by the working people. The following three decades had been a period of phenomenal industrial expansion in England. Militancy was fiercely repressed, but while the franchise was progressively enlarged and the conditions of the skilled workers were improved through the work of the Trades Unions, the lot of the unskilled poor remained unbearable. When, in the late 1870s, financial depression began to cause widespread distress, older radical ideas began to revive, partly under the influence of political refugees from Russia, Germany, Austria and France, many of whom were inspired by the writings of Marx.

The practical, moral and intellectual failure of Marxism, so evident at the close of the twentieth century, inevitably reflects on the direction Morris's thought was now to take. It was natural however that he should be drawn to the most powerful critic of nineteenth century industrial society, and it is in this context that we should view Morris's reading of *Capital*. Nothing shows him more clearly as a man of his age.

Morris and Marx agreed that man is essentially a maker and that the essence of his human life is embodied in the things he makes: a house, a tapestry, a wallpaper. For Marx, these items were 'the objectification of man's species life'. In the ideal world of Marx's early thought, such products could be freely made and kept or disposed of as the maker desired. Love and trust would be the basis on which objects were both created and distributed. Co-operation would be the foundation of human relationships, and men would appreciate the natural qualities of the things they produced rather than merely their financial worth.

All of this was deeply agreeable to Morris, but Marx was profoundly to influence him by his searching analysis of how, in a capitalist society, this free creation and exchange has been denied man. What is produced now belongs not to the maker but to those who employ him. Workers no longer control what they make and, indeed, find what they produce is used to keep them in poverty and dependence. They have become 'alienated' from their productions and so from their essential humanity. Cooperation has been replaced by bargaining and exchange. In such a world, money has become the dominant power, and men begin to worship this alienated essence of their true being, thereby losing their humanity. This is a profound insight into the working of the market place. It helped to clarify some of Morris's deepest intuitions and led him in turn to becoming one of the most powerful writers on the effects of alienation in the English language.

Owing to the extensive use of machinery and to division of labour, the work of the proletarians has lost all individual character, and, consequently, all charm for the workman. He becomes an appendage of the machine, and it is only the most simple, most monotonous, and most easily acquired knack, that is required of him. Hence, the cost of production of a workman is restricted, almost entirely, to the means of subsistence that he requires for his maintenance, and for the propagation of his race. But the price of a commodity, and therefore also of labour, is equal to its cost of production. In proportion, therefore, as the repulsiveness of the work increases, the wage decreases. Nay more, in proportion as the use of machinery and division of

Marx's analysis of alienation had a decisive effect on Morris's thought.

labour increases, in the same proportion the burden of toil also increases, whether by prolongation of the working hours, by increase of the work exacted in a given time or by increased speed of the machinery, etc.

Neither Morris nor Marx however believed that the market-place was indeed man's natural home. As we have seen, Morris's objection to Victorian industrial society was precisely its woeful artificiality when compared to what he thought of as the more cooperative world of the Middle Ages. Marx also believed that the marketplace was only a stage in the development of history whose ultimate and logical goal was the freeing of mankind.

For Marx, mankind was most fully represented by the working classes, the proletariat, whose total deprivation gave them this universal character. Artificially beggared by capitalism, they were yet bound by an inexorable logic to free themselves through revolution, and in turn destroy the capitalists who had made them what they were.

Revolution appeared as the only answer to alienation to both Morris and Marx.

The proletariat goes through various stages of development. With its birth begins its struggle with the bourgeoisie. At first the contest is carried on by individual labourers, then by the work-people of a factory, then by the operatives of one trade, in one locality, against the individual bourgeois who directly exploits them. They direct their attacks not against the bourgeois conditions of production, but against the instruments of production themselves; they destroy imported wares that compete with their labour, they smash to pieces machinery, they set factories ablaze, they seek to restore by force the vanished status of the workman of the Middle Ages.

As Morris was to show in *News From Nowhere*, in this new world, private property will have been abolished, 'alienation between men and their products' will disappear and fully human beings will, in Morris's words: 'regain control of exchange, production and the mode of their mutual relationships.' The state will have withered away and with it greed, envy and corruption. Since Marx also believed that it is the material conditions of society that create consciousness rather than the reverse, a new human awareness will dawn with these new material conditions. At the end of history, communism will allow men to pass on to what Engels called 'a really human morality,' a mental and moral state beautifully portrayed in *News From Nowhere* by the character of Ellen.

Whatever may have happened since, *Capital* remains one of the great critiques of the undesirable consequences of capitalism, and the first volume of the work is a carefully documented nightmare of Victorian England 'dripping from head to foot from every pore, with blood and dirt'. It also offers a pungent analysis of many of the contemporary evils which roused Morris's wrath.

A number of these were voiced in Morris's own lectures at this time. In 'Art, Wealth, and Riches', first delivered in 1883, for example, he inveighed against the division of labour which ensures that the workman 'is part of a machine, and has one set of unchanging tasks to do, and when he has once learned them, the more regularly and with the less thought he does them, the more valuable he is'. Morris saw very clearly that change must come but was as yet wary of revolution: 'how good it were to destroy all that must be destroyed gradually and with good grace!' This was a view that earned him the tart criticism of Engels who considered Morris 'a settled sentimental socialist.'

And among those evils, I do, and must always, believe will fall that one which last year I told you that I accounted the greatest of all evils, the heaviest of all slaveries; that evil of the greater part of the population being engaged for by far the most part of their lives in work, which at the best cannot interest them, or develop their faculties, and at the worst (and that is the commonest, too) is mere unmitigated slavish toil, only to be wrung out of them by the sternest compulsion, a toil which they shirk all they can—small blame to them. And this toil degrades them into less than men: and they will some day come to know it, and cry out to be made men again, and art only can do it, and redeem them from this slavery; and I say once more that this is her highest and most glorious end and aim; and it is in her struggle to attain to it that she will most surely purify herself, and quicken her own aspirations towards perfection.

'Mere unmitigated slavish toil' was the lot of the poor in England and Morris repeatedly attacked it.

It was, appropriately enough, in Oxford and at a meeting gathered under the auspices of Ruskin among others that Morris first publicly declared himself a socialist. 'Art and Democracy' (1883) is one of his most stirring lectures and contains a number of his most important themes.

'I am "one of the people called Socialists",' Morris declared. 'I hold that the condition of competition between man and man is bestial only, and that of association human.' Capitalism, he stated, meant degradation and, in the end, the collapse of civilisation. But if capitalism was destroying the true relationship of man to man, it was also destroying the environment in which he lived. 'A love of dirt and ugliness for its own sake' seemed to be spreading over the entire country, not just in London and Manchester but even amid the medieval beauty of Oxford.

That commercialism was the chief polluter of the English countryside was a point Morris repeatedly made with a passion that seems ever more relevant to our own times.

Nor can I, an artist, think last or least of the outward effects which betoken this rule of the wretched anarchy of Commercial war. Think of the spreading sore of London swallowing up with its loathsomeness field and wood and heath without mercy and without hope, mocking our feeble efforts to deal even with its minor evils of smoke-laden sky and befouled river: the black horror and reckless squalor of our manufacturing districts, so dreadful to the senses which are unused to them that it is ominous for the future of the race that any man can live among it in tolerable cheerfulness: nay in the open country itself the thrusting aside by miserable jerry-built brick and slate of the solid grey dwellings that are still scattered about, fit emblems in their cheery but beautiful simplicity of the yeomen of the English field, whose destruction at the hands of yet young Commercial war was lamented so touchingly by the highminded More and the valiant Latimer. Everywhere in short the change from old to new involving one certainty, whatever else may be doubtful, a worsening of the aspect of the country.

The expensively educated classes to whom Morris was talking lacked, he said, any interest in life '. . . except, it may be, the cultivation of unhappiness as a fine art'. The proletariat, meanwhile, were being reduced to an alienated and bestial life by the use of the machine not as a means of reducing the burden of soul-destroying labour—something of which Morris invariably approved—but by its exploitation purely for profit. It is the lot of the poor '. . . to expend all the divine energy of man in competing for something less than a dog's lodging and a dog's food,' while the rich sit uselessly by.

From The Lesser Arts.

I do not want art for a few, any more than education for a few, or freedom for a few.

The sense of social crisis carries the lecture along with great force, yet the plea is still for amelioration rather than revolution. It was the middle classes, the young men seated before him, who would determine whether civilisation would be saved or die. Morris concluded by urging them to action and pleading for donations. All the dons save Ruskin were appalled.

At the start of the following year, Morris delivered two of his most famous lectures: 'Useful Work versus Useless Toil' and 'Art and Socialism'. Both show the strong influence of Marx and Morris's own far from servile interpretation of his writings.

'Useful Work versus Useless Toil', first delivered in 1884, for example, opens with a lucid account of the inequities of the class system and an inspiring description—clearly the result of personal experience—of the true delights of labour when these are free and unalienated.

It is from this profound appreciation of the joys of work - of all Morris's contributions to socialist theory the one that is perhaps the most fully imagined—that there stemmed his call for social change. He was fully aware of the moral squalor caused by capitalists hoarding the surplus value of the objects produced by their workers. He believed that this was both undesirable and unnecessary. Social change should establish community, balanced work, fair reward, leisure and something that for Morris was of exceptional importance: the simple, modest demand that we should take 'a pleasurable interest in all the details of life'. In the utopian world of *News from Nowhere*, this becomes a theme handled with a poetic subtlety that Morris is too infrequently given credit for. Indeed, the lecture as a whole points forward to that delightful work.

Above: *A photograph of William Morris taken in the mid 1880s.*

So I will say that I believe there are two virtues much needed in modern life, if it is ever to become sweet; and I am quite sure that they are absolutely necessary in the sowing the seed of an *art which is to be made by the people and for the people, as a happiness to the maker and the user*. These virtues are honesty, and simplicity of life. To make my meaning clearer I will name the opposing vice of the second of these—luxury to wit. Also I mean by honesty, the careful and eager giving his due to every man, the determination not to gain by any man's loss, which in my experience is not a common virtue.

If Morris was a shrewd analyst of alienated labour he was also eloquent in his praise of the art that would salve men's lives.

Variety of work is the next point, and a most important one. To compel a man to do day after day the same task, without any

In Useful Work versus Useless Toil *Morris argued for variety in labour.*

hope of escape or change, means nothing short of turning his life into a prison-torment. Nothing but the tyranny of profit-grinding makes this necessary. A man might easily learn and practise at least three crafts, varying sedentary occupation with outdoor—occupation calling for the exercise of strong bodily energy for work in which the mind had more to do. There are few men, for instance, who would not wish to spend part of their lives in the most necessary and pleasantest of all work—cultivating the earth. One thing which will make this variety of employment possible will be the form that education will take in a socially ordered community. At present all education is directed towards the end of fitting people to take their places in the hierarchy of commerce—these as masters, those as workmen. The education of the masters is more ornamental than that of the workmen, but it is commercial still; and even at the ancient universities learning is but little regarded, unless it can in the long run be made *to pay*. Due education is a totally different thing from this, and concerns itself in finding out what different people are fit for, and helping them along the road which they are inclined to take. In a duly ordered society, therefore, young people would be taught such handicrafts as they had a turn for as a part of their education, the discipline of their minds and bodies; and adults would also have opportunities of learning in the same schools, for the development of individual capacities would be of all things chiefly aimed at by education, instead, as now, the subordination of all capacities to the great end of 'money-making' for oneself—or one's master. The amount of talent, and even genius, which the present system crushes, and which would be drawn out by such a system, would make our daily work easy and interesting.

Morris's vision of unity was not however being put into practice by the comrades who were supposed to be helping to bring it about. In particular, Henry Hyndman, the leading figure of The Social Democratic Foundation, was a quarrelsome and often devious 'political boss' of remarkable energy and persistence. He wanted the Federation to enter candidates for elections, while Morris, uncertain of the real use of small scale advances on particular issues, now believed that the chief function of the Federation should be to educate the people towards revolution. He considered anything else threatened the danger of assimilation into the middle classes. He consequently devoted his enormous energies to lecturing, to setting up a branch of the Federation in Hammersmith and to working on and subsidising *Justice*, the country's first socialist weekly started in 1884.

Justice included one article by Morris of particular interest: 'A Factory as it Might Be'. Here he offered an idealistic picture of future industrial conditions, of pleasant factories set in gardens and managed in a way mindful of the dangers of pollution. The buildings were no longer 'temples of over-crowding and adulteration and over-work' but beautiful places fitted up with amenities for the workers. Labour in such an environment would be satisfying and honourable while, in tune with his often given opinion on the subject, 'machines of the most ingenious and best-approved kinds will be used when necessary'. Such machines will be employed to ease labour and not to accumulate more and more profit. Nor will mindless machine-tending be the sole occupation during the four hours of daily labour. Variety of work and education, a shared interest in developing manufacturing skills and the practice of the fine arts will all be encouraged. The result will be products of beauty and use made by people for whom work is no longer a burden.

Left: Henry Myers Hyndman, the founder of the Democratic Federation, is pictured on the left of this photograph taken c. 1907.

135/2

Agitate.   Educate.   Organize.

THE

DEMOCRATIC FEDERATION,

HAMMERSMITH BRANCH.

Temporary Premises : —Kelmscott House, Upper Mall, Hammersmith.

Fellow Workers,

You are invited to join this branch, and help in spreading the principles of Socialism : some of you may be frightened at this word, and naturally so ; since you have been misled and told that it means disorder and violence.

But what is the real truth ?   This, that as society is now arranged there is necessarily a constant war between *Capital*, or the rich men who make profits out of work without working themselves, and *Labour*, or the poor men, who produce every thing, and have no more share in what they produce than is necessary to keep them alive and at work while they live.

Into these two classes, rich and poor, all society is divided, and whatever profits the rich make they make at the expense of the poor, or those who are called the working classes : so also any bettering of life which the poor, or working classes, can gain, they gain at the expense of the rich.

This is *war*, and bears with it all the waste and ruin of *war;* so that while the rich enslave the poor, they themselves are not happy, and are always trying to ruin each other.

SOCIALISM will end this war by abolishing all classes, and making every one work for the common good ; so that while every man will have the full fruits of his own labour, of which he is now deprived, he will benefit every one else by his work : this change will get rid of bad-housing, under feeding, over-work, and ignorance. and give every one a fair chance of health and happiness.

PEACE, WELL-BEING AND ORDER, FOR ALL THEREFORE ARE THE REAL AIMS OF SOCIALISM.

To obtain these the one thing necessary is the COMBINATION of the workers : they, who create all wealth, must learn to undertand that socialism means the change from fighting each with each for life like beasts, to working together for life like men : they must get to know each other, and agree together that this change MUST be made, and then it *will* be made.

Working-men of Hammersmith, come to the Branch and learn about those matters which to you are all important : join the Branch of the Democratic Federation, so that you may combine for real freedom, for a life fit for human beings.

Members of the Branch meet every Monday at 8.15 p.m. for business at Kelmscott House, Upper Mall, (notice the board on the gate). Visitors are invited. All information can be obtained there as to meetings, lectures and literature of the Democratic Federation. Lectures of the Hammersmith Branch will be duly announced in "Justice," the organ of the Social Democracy.

All communications to be addressed to the Secretary, Hammersmith Branch of the Democratic Federation, 3, Hammersmith Terrace, W.

Read "JUSTICE," the organ of the Social Democracy, ONE PENNY WEEKLY, *to be had of all newsmen.*

Churchman, Printer, Hammersmith.

Now as to the work, first of all it will be useful, and, therefore, honourable and honoured; because there will be no temptation to make mere useless toys, since there will be no rich men cudgelling their brains for means for spending superfluous money, and consequently no 'organisers of labour' pandering to degrading follies for the sake of profit, wasting their intelligence and energy in contriving snares for cash in the shape of trumpery which they themselves heartily despise. Nor will the work turn out trash; there will be no millions of poor to make a market for wares which no one would choose to use if he were not driven to do so; everyone will be able to afford things good of their kind, and, as will be shown hereafter, will have knowledge of goods enough to reject what is not excellent; coarse and rough wares may be made for rough or temporary purposes, but they will openly proclaim themselves for what they are; adulteration will be unknown.

Furthermore, machines of the most ingenious and best-approved kinds will be used when necessary, but will be used simply to save human labour; nor, indeed, could they be used for anything else in such well-ordered work as we are thinking about; since, profit being dead, there would be no temptation to pile up wares whose apparent value as articles of *use*, their conventional value as such, does not rest on the necessities or reasonable desires of men for such things, but on artificial habits forced on the public by the craving of the capitalists for fresh and ever fresh profit; these things have no real value as things to be used, and their conventional (let us say sham) utility value has been the breed of their value, as articles of exchange for profit, in a society founded on profit-mongering.

Well, the manufacture of useless goods, whether harmful luxuries for the rich or disgraceful make-shifts for the poor, having come to an end, and we still being in possession of the machines once used for mere profit-grinding, but now used only for saving human labour, it follows that much less labour will be necessary for each workman; all the more as we are going to get rid of all non-workers, and busy-idle people; so that the working time of each member of our factory will be very short, say, to be much within the mark, four hours a day.

Morris was not, as is often supposed, an outright enemy of the machine. He saw its great potential for liberating man from drudgery and praised this.

Opposite: *Manifesto of the Social Democratic Federation.*

Our epoch has invented machines which would have appeared wild dreams to the men of past ages, and of those machines we have as yet *made no use.*

They are called 'labour-saving' machines—a commonly used phrase which implies what we expect of them; but we do not get what we expect. What they really do is to reduce the skilled labourer to the ranks of the unskilled, to increase the number of the 'reserve army of labour'—that is, to increase the

What Morris attacked was the ease with which the machine could become merely an instrument for making money and so enslave workers into a capitalist society in which they were helpless slaves.

precariousness of life among the workers and to intensify the labour of those who serve the machines (as slaves their masters). All this they do by the way, while they pile up the profits of the employers of labour, or force them to expand those profits in bitter commercial war with each other. In a true society these miracles of ingenuity would be for the first time used for minimizing the amount of time spent in unattractive labour, which by their means might be so reduced as to be but a very light burden on each individual. All the more as these machines would most certainly be very much improved when it was no longer a question as to whether their improvement would 'pay' the individual, but rather whether it would benefit the community.

This is a vision of an ideal, of course. But what of Morris's own status as a factory owner? He was keenly aware of the difficult position he was obliged to face as both a socialist and an industrial employer. For a brief period he seems even to have considered selling his business and living on a weekly wage like any member of the proletariat. This was clearly impractical, as was a wholesale system of profit-sharing. While some of the senior workmen at Merton Abbey were indeed placed on profit-related bonuses, Morris realised that to extend this system to all his employees would not be to bring socialism about since they would still be enmeshed in a capitalist society. In Morris's words: 'an employer by giving up his industrial profit of the goods he gets made would not be able to put his workmen in their proper position: they would be exploited by others though not by him.'

What Morris could do was to ensure that pay and working conditions were reasonable. The latter was certainly appreciated. Of work at Merton Abbey, George Wardle wrote: 'there seems to be nothing to say except that it was altogether delightful.' Mackail, too, described the cotton fabrics bleaching among the buttercups and trout leaping outside the windows of the long, cheerful room that housed the carpet looms.

Yet Morris himself was clearly aware that conditions at Merton Abbey were not idyllic. One visitor recorded how, when Morris had led her through the textile weaving sheds and out again into the fresh air, he '. . . reverted with a sigh to the great problem, and asked why men should be imprisoned thus for a lifetime in the midst of such deafening chatter in order to earn a bare subsistence, which the average professional man pockets in comfortable ease'. When we come to examine the conditions under which the tapestry weavers worked, this problem will be seen at its most acute.

Even under the management of a committed socialist it appeared that there was inevitably exploitation and a lack of that delight in making which was so central to Morris's thought. For all his repeated insistence that art should be 'a joy to the maker and to the user,' much of the work at Merton Abbey as well as among Morris's sub-contractors was mechanical. The ideal conditions imagined to belong to the Middle Ages could not be easily recreated. As Morris himself declared:

> I have got to understand thoroughly the manner of work under which the Art of the Middle Ages was done, and that that is the *only* manner of work which can turn out popular art, only to discover that it is impossible to work in that manner in a profit grinding society . . . impossible to do more than to ensure the *designer* (mostly myself) some pleasure in his art by getting him to understand the qualities of materials and the happy chances of the processes. Except with a small part of the more artistic side of the work, I could not do anything (or at least but little) to give this pleasure to the workmen, because I should have had to change their method of work so utterly that I should have disqualified them from earning their living elsewhere.

Below: *Handblock printing at Merton Abbey.*

This is the heart of the paradox. On the one hand Morris looked back to the Middle Ages for his ideal of labour. On the other he looked forward to an imagined future, equally idealistic, where the workman would again be free. In his own age he was obliged to be a Janus figure. He insisted on such mechanical and repetitive work as hand block printing while his designs were in many respects suited to the infinite multiplication of mechanical reproduction. As a socialist, he saw the machine as a means of freeing men for a fuller life in which they could practise the very arts he so praised. The ideal of the Middle Ages could only finally be realised, he believed, in a future created by the revolution.

Morris's description of the socialist ideal.

Well, surely Socialism can offer you something in the place of all that. It can; it can offer you peace and friendship instead of war. We might live utterly without national rivalries, acknowledging that while it is best for those who feel that they naturally form a community under one name to govern themselves, yet that no community in civilization should feel that it had interests opposed to any other, their economical condition being at any rate similar; so that any citizen of one community could fall to work and live without disturbance of his life when he was in a foreign country, and would fit into his place quite naturally; so that all civilized nations would form one great community, agreeing together as to the kind and amount of production and distribution needed; working at such and such production where it could be best produced; avoiding waste by all means. Please to think of the amount of waste which they would avoid, how much such a revolution would add to the wealth of the world! What creature on earth would be harmed by such a revolution? Nay, would not everybody be the better for it? And what hinders it? I will tell you presently.

But if Socialism and the revolution were the only hope for the arts, there were deep divisions in the Social Democratic Foundation itself. Both temperamentally and ideologically, Morris and Hyndman were unsuited to each other. Further, the backstabbing and recrimination, the constant battle between purism and action—briefly, the capacity for rancorous self-division that almost inevitably accompanies minority radical groups—put Morris in a position he could no longer tolerate. Eventually, in December 1884, he led a majority of the executive members out of the Federation and set up the Socialist League. With him went, among others, the unscrupulous Edward Aveling and his lover Eleanor Marx; Ernest Belfort Bax; Thomas Binning, a compositor; and John Mahon, an engineer and the League's Secretary.

Their manifesto proclaimed their intentions: 'Fellow Citizens—We come before you as a body advocating the principles of Revolutionary International Socialism: that is, we seek a change in the basis of Society—a change which would destroy the distinctions of classes and nationalities.' Their magazine *The Commonweal*, first published in 1885, was designed to educate the masses towards the revolution.

Left: *Advertising wrapper for* The Commonweal.

Below: *Morris is clearly distinguishable by his white beard in this photograph of the Hammersmith Branch of the Socialist League. May Morris is the second seated figure on the left in the front row.*

'The next six years,' wrote May Morris, 'are a long story of lecturing, travelling, office and editorial work, and that most difficult of all tasks, keeping the peace among people of different temperaments: people eager and impetuous and most of them honest in their aims, but possessing a positive genius for misunderstanding each other.' What sustained Morris, aside from the vast resources of his natural energy, was the profound depth of his socialist conviction, a belief in the coming of the revolution which was now Messianic in its fervour. 'One must turn to hope,' Morris wrote to Georgina Burne-Jones, 'and only in one direction do I see it—on the road to Revolution: everything else is gone now. And now at last when the corruption of society seems complete, there is arising a definite conception of a new order.'

Morris successfully managed to keep the League from colliding too violently with the Federation. A year after its first issue, *The Commonweal* became a weekly and enjoyed a circulation of between two and three thousand. Morris himself wrote continuously for it, many of his pieces such as that on a case of white lead poisoning having a vigorous, embittered realism that is remarkably trenchant. The paper also published *The Pilgrims of Hope*

An article in the Commonweal *for October 1886 shows that Morris had an accurate and detailed knowledge of the evils of the capitalist society about him.*

A case of white-lead poisoning reported in the press this week is worth a little notice by workmen generally. Stripped of verbiage it amounts to this, that a man was killed by being compelled to work in a place where white-lead was flying about, and that no precautions were taken to prevent his dying speedily. A shilling-a-week extra was the handsome sum given to the poor man thus murdered in compensation for his being killed. It is quite impossible that the man's employers did not know the risk he ran of this speedier death, and the certainty of his being poisoned later, and yet all that the jury durst say about the matter was 'to express a hope that Mr Lakeman (the factory inspector) would be able to make representations to the Home Office with reference to the case, to show the necessity for some extra precautions being taken for people working in mixing factories'.

Yet further this is only an exaggerated example of the way in which the lives of working-people are played with. Under present conditions, almost the whole labour imposed by civilization on the 'lower classes' is unwholesome; that is to say that people's lives are shortened by it; and yet because we don't see people's throats cut before our eyes we think nothing of it.

(1885), a long and sometimes rather commonplace socialist epic set in the Paris Commune. The work has a strong autobiographical element in which Morris tells how a man is betrayed by his wife who falls in love with his best friend. It also offers a vivid picture—and one suggested again in a number of Morris's letters—of the dispiriting moments in the life of a socialist campaigner:

Dull and dirty the room. Just over the chairman's chair
Was a bust, a Quaker's face with nose cocked up in the air;
There were common prints on the wall of the heads of the party
   fray,
And Manzzini dark and lean amidst them gone astray.
Some thirty men we were of the kind that I knew full well,
Listless, rubbed down to the type of our easy-going hell.
My heart sank down as I entered, and wearily there I sat
While the chairman strove to end his maunder of this and of
   that
And partly shy he seemed, and partly indeed ashamed
Of the grizzled man beside him as his name to us he named.
He rose, thickset and short, and dressed in shabby blue,
And even as he began it seemed as though I knew
The thing he was going to say, though I never heard it before.
He spoke, were it well, were it ill, as though a message he
   bore,
A word that he could not refrain from many a million men . . .
But they sat and made no sign, and two of the glibber kind
Stood up to jeer and carp, his fiery words to blind.
. . . I rose ere the meeting was done,
And gave him my name and my faith—and I was the only one.

There were successes nonetheless. Open air meetings were often well attended, and by 1886 membership of the League had risen to seven hundred. There were nine London branches and nearly a dozen in the provinces. Between 1885–86, Morris himself lectured one hundred and twenty times, travelled the Midlands, Scotland, Dublin and East Anglia (often translating Homer as he went) while he also acted as the League's treasurer, the editor of its journal and the most influential figure on its executive. Education for revolution became an ever more insistent theme. As he told the *Daily News*:

Discontent is not enough, though it is natural and inevitable. The discontented must know what they are aiming at when they overthrow the old order of things. My belief is that the old order can only be overthrown by force; and for that reason it is all the more important that the revolution . . . should not be an ignorant, but an educated revolution.

Such statements brought an inevitable reaction. In 1885, the police violently broke up a meeting of the International Working Men's Club of Tottenham Court Road. A defence committee was formed with Morris as its Treasurer and three policemen were sent to trial at the Old Bailey. Open air meetings continued to be harassed nonetheless. The Social Democratic Foundation was involved in an incident at Whitechapel. Some of its members were arrested for 'obstruction' and there was uproar in the court when the middle class prisoners were fined £2 each while the tailor Lewis Lyons was sentenced to two month's hard labour. Morris was involved in the affray, brought before the magistrate but discharged. Although Lyons's sentence was later quashed on appeal, the action of the police won the socialists much public sympathy.

Morris was well aware of the usefulness of this. The trade recession however meant that distress and discontent were rife. The Social Democratic Foundation began agitating among the unemployed. As a mass meeting in Trafalgar Square marched up Pall Mall, so it was jeered by the clubmen. Stones were hurled and windows were broken. The incensed crowd surged up St James's and looted the shops in Piccadilly. Morris, deeply disturbed, wrote in *The Commonweal* that this was an 'aimless' incident even if it was a first step on the path to revolution. 'At the risk of being misunderstood by hotheads,' he continued, 'I say that our business is more than ever *Education.*'

Violence was mounting. In Birmingham, Norwich and Leicester other members of the unemployed demonstrated and rioted. The police became more active in breaking up socialist meetings, and Morris regularly appeared in court to stand surety for those arrested. His own speeches were also becoming more challenging. At the corner of Bell Street off the Edgware Road, for instance, he declared he was maintaining the rights of free speech for socialists. The police asked him to desist. He refused, declaring that the conditions of the working people were intolerable and that 'society must be turned downside up'. He called on the crowd to prepare for revolution and was promptly arrested for obstruction.

What happened in court is a vivid reflection of the inequality of Victorian society. The magistrate, clearly embarrassed by the presence of Morris in the dock, turned to address him as one gentleman to another, stating that '. . . as a gentleman, he would at once see, when it was pointed out to him, that such meetings were a nuisance, and would desist from taking part in them'. He then fined Morris 1s 0d. Morris's colleagues, however, not being part of this comfortable middle class understanding, were each fined £20 and bound over for a year. They refused to pay the fines and were jailed for two months.

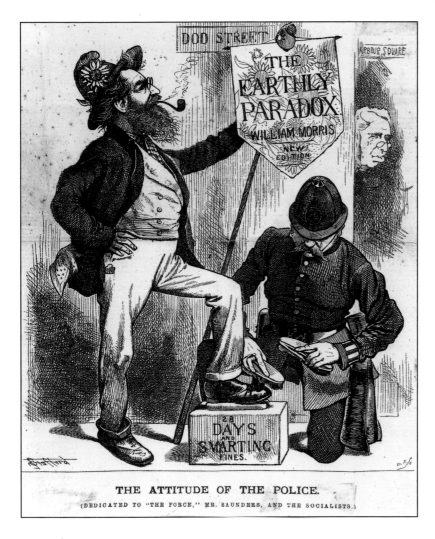

THE ATTITUDE OF THE POLICE.

(DEDICATED TO "THE FORCE," MR. SAUNDERS, AND THE SOCIALISTS.)

Left: *This cartoon suggests the lenient attitude taken towards Morris by the authorities at the time when he was most actively campaigning for revolutionary socialism.*

By the autumn of 1887, matters were reaching a crisis. Meetings in Trafalgar Square, though cleared by the police, were held almost daily. The greatest imperial power in the world seemed threatened from within. The Commissioner of Police for London banned further meetings on the ground that the Square itself was Crown property. While the newspapers largely rallied to his support, the *Pall Mall Gazette* stood up for free speech and accused the authorities of provocation. Morris at once wrote to the editor proposing to set up a Law and Liberty League. Others joined him, and the Federation of Radical Clubs called a demonstration in Trafalgar Square on Sunday 13 November.

'Bloody Sunday', as it has come to be called, was one of the turning points in British socialism. Between 80,000 and 100,000 people gathered to protest at the treatment of an Irish MP. Trafalgar Square itself was cordoned off by police in ranks four deep. Mounted police struck out with batons at the gathering crowds.

Further away, three hundred foot soldiers with fixed bayonets and twenty rounds of ammunition each stood ready, supported by a battalion of Life Guards.

Right: *On 13 November, 1887, the great protesting crowds that had gathered in Trafalgar Square were dispersed by police and mounted soldiers. 'Bloody Sunday' as the incident has come to be called was recreated by Morris in* News from Nowhere *when he came to describe the hour of the socialist revolution.*

Morris himself, along with the radical Annie Besant, had told his band of the Socialist League that '...whenever free speech was attempted to be put down, it was their bounden duty to resist the attempt by every means in their power'. They must, however 'press on into the Square like orderly people and good citizens'.

They then marched from Clerkenwell in a contingent of some five thousand people and got as far as Seven Dials. Morris, realising that there might be trouble, had moved to the head of the column. What followed may be told in his own words:

> The police struck right and left like what they were, soldiers attacking an enemy, amid wild shrieks of hatred from the women who came from the slums on our left. The band-instruments were captured, the banners and flags destroyed, there was no rallying point and no possibility of rallying, and all the people composing our strong column could do was to struggle into the Square as helpless units. I confess I was amazed at the rapidity of the thing and the ease with which the military organisation got its victory. I could see that numbers were of no avail unless led by a band of men acting in concert and each knowing his part.

They were an untrained crowd facing a small army. The result was inevitably brutal though not a massacre. Unarmed women and children were beaten as the fashionable looked on and applauded. Two hundred wounded protesters were sent to hospital. Three died of their wounds.

At a demonstration a week later, Alfred Linnell fell beneath a mounted policeman in Northumberland Avenue. Morris wrote 'A Death Song' which was sold at Linnell's funeral to help support his wife and children. Morris was also a pall-bearer in the great procession that marched in the pouring rain to Bow Cemetery.

The power of capitalism had been revealed. For Morris's friend Bernard Shaw it was a clear indication that socialism must be brought about by other means, while Morris himself was obliged to recognise that successful revolution was now a distant prospect indeed.

Nor was the League itself in a healthy state. Though by 1887 membership had peaked at about 1000, the branches were divided and weakening as time was spent on 'bombastic revolutionary talk.' Morris himself was beginning to understand that his original opposition to parliamentary tactics and Trade Union activities might have been too extreme. He was also considerably impressed by a miner's strike in Northumberland that year organised by Mahon. Nonetheless, at the end of 1887, Mahon himself left the League after a resolution in favour of putting up parliamentary candidates was defeated. Bax's Croydon branch and Aveling's group in Bloomsbury followed him a year later.

Those remaining in the League were of a decidedly anarchist tendency. Morris found this distasteful and irrelevant, just as he did the great advances towards state socialism now being engineered by Shaw and the Fabians as well as Keir Hardie and the Independent Labour Party. By 1889, Morris had largely abandoned hope for the League. *The Commonweal* was being superseded by more practical papers, while the anarchists themselves eventually removed Morris from his editorial post. At the end of the year, he withdrew from the League which was now without its chief financial sponsor.

In the words of Bernard Shaw: 'Morris, who had been holding the League up by the scruff of the neck, opened his hand, whereupon it dropped like a stone into the sea, leaving only a little wreckage to come to the surface occasionally, a demand for bail at the police court or a small loan.' Though the League had been influential in the early days of socialist propaganda, it had now been overtaken by state socialists whose views Morris could not wholly endorse but who held nonetheless the key to the future. In 1892, for example, the hugely augmented unions helped achieve the election of three Independent Labour Members to Parliament. Morris, cheered though he was and hugely sustaining though his example had been, was left to preach revolution on the dank streets of Hammersmith.

UTOPIAN DREAMER

Throughout the period of his most active political campaigning and into his last years, Morris's experiments with design continued unabated. Techniques learned in the early days of the Firm were largely maintained, carpet making and tapestry weaving were raised to new heights, an interest in printing and book design gave new directions to a great craft, while friendships with a range of younger men stimulated a flourishing of design in which Britain led the world.

This range of activity was made possible by a number of factors. Morris's finances were now eased by no longer having to fund the Socialist League, though he still helped to support his Hammersmith Socialist Society. The management of the Firm was largely in the hands of the Smith brothers, while J. H. Dearle supervised the Merton Abbey works. Finally, highly talented assistants such as May Morris and Dearle himself were responsible for designs in the Morris mode in those areas where Morris himself was now content to contribute less.

This is particularly evident in embroidery. May Morris had taken over the embroidery section of the Firm in 1885, married Henry Halliday Sparling, then Secretary of the Socialist League, and moved into 8 Hammersmith Terrace where the embroiderers worked in the drawing room under May's supervision. Among these very talented women were Lily, the sister of the poet W.B. Yeats, Mary de Morgan and Mrs George Jack, the wife of the Firm's furniture designer.

The patterns on which these women worked were transferred from pricked paper onto the background fabric, and when not sold to customers in this state or partially worked, were completed in Hammersmith Terrace. While May's designs clearly reflect the influence of her father (a man for whom she preserved an attitude bordering on reverence) they also reveal an original use of received motifs. A panel of flowers and cockatoos designed and embroidered by her in about 1895, for example, has a flickering liveliness of movement beyond anything Morris himself achieved in this mode. May's skills are further revealed in the bed

Opposite: *Pigskin binding for the Kelmscott Chaucer.*

and wall hangings which her admirer George Bernard Shaw described as 'glowing fruit-forests'.

May, indeed, was a considerable personality. She seems to have managed her group of embroiderers with fairness, tact and generosity. Her own embroidery skills were considerable and led her to publish a number of articles on the subject as well as her book *Decorative Needlework*.

May had also sewn banners for her father's political groups, was herself a Socialist and became sufficiently interested in the status of women to found the Women's Guild of Art as a 'centre and a bond for the women who were doing decorative work in all the various crafts represented at that time'. May also edited her father's writings, while her influence on embroidery through her activities as a teacher and lecturer in England and the United States was considerable. In her time, May was recognised as an outstanding figure and, on her death in 1935, she received tributes from many notable Fabians and figures in the art world.

If the quality of May's involvement in the embroidery department of the Firm raised its output to heights of achievement it had not perhaps reached before, the Firm's stained glass in the 1880s and after shows a distinct deterioration.

This was partly due to the fact that Morris took little part in its supervision. Indeed, after the move to Merton Abbey, the firing of the glass was left to outside firms. But it is also true that as Burne-Jones's own style developed towards the imitation of Renaissance models, so his feeling for the inherent qualities of the medium and for medieval examples especially began to be lost. Areas of colour became broader and paler, while dynamic contrasts were less assured. In addition, the figures are increasingly sentimental until new influences finally brought about a revived style and the great achievements of Burne-Jones's old age. These windows date from after Morris's death however, and in the meantime the repetition of old designs led to a slackening and sad diminution of quality.

After 1890, Morris continued to produce a number of designs for wallpaper. Some, such as the *Triple Net*, are rather rigid, while others such as the *Hammersmith* and *Lechlade*, are somewhat lacking in originality. The best designs, such as *Bachelor's Button*, are finely inventive in their combination of simply drawn and often naturalistic motifs juxtaposed to the swirling arabesques of acanthus leaves.

But if Morris himself had now past his greatest period of wallpaper designing, John Henry Dearle developed many of his ideas with considerable force. Dearle had originally been taken on in 1878 as an assistant in the Oxford Street shop. From there he was transferred to the glass-painting studio, and so impressed was Morris by his natural abilities that he selected Dearle to help with the early tapestry experiments at Queen Square. Later, Dearle contributed to many of the Firm's designing activities: to wallpapers, to woven and printed textiles, to carpets and to tapestries.

Like May Morris, Dearle's achievements have been overshadowed by those of his master. This is unfortunate since he was a considerable designer in his own right. The magnificent *Compton* of 1896, for example, is now attributed to him . Indeed, this is one of the finest of the Firm's designs: a marvellous arrangement of poppies and tulips, speedwell, pimpernel and the most vividly articulated open honeysuckle flowers. There is a strong and sensuous drama to the whole, much helped by the placing of the flower heads on a dark background, as well as by the suggestion of the Middle Eastern designs Dearle so favoured.

Above: *A portrait of Henry Dearle.*

Compton was produced both as a wallpaper and as a printed textile, and it was perhaps as a textile designer that Dearle was most distinguished. Attributing designs to Dearle is confused by much of his work being loosely assigned to Morris in contemporary catalogues when it is probably the name of the Firm that is being referred to. However, Dearle's particular qualities are now coming to be distinguished and appreciated. He was a highly skilled designer, craftsman and administrator whose work, though rarely if ever free from Morris's commanding influence, was of vital importance to the continuing life of the Firm as Morris's interests developed into other areas.

While Dearle's early work shows obvious signs of inexperience and a heavy dependence on Morris, by 1889 he was responsible for virtually all the Firm's textile designs. In the field of printed cottons especially, the early Dearle showed a marked preference for a sinuous vertical motif, often lightly decorated with naturalistic or formal elements, which was then placed on a ground of prettily worked flowers. This is seen at its best in *Daffodil*, where the rhythms of the vertical elements are delightfully echoed in the background flowers which give the textile its name. Pointed buds (a favourite motif of Dearle's) then provide a lively sense of counterpoint. Later designs such as *Eden* show how strongly Dearle could adapt Middle Eastern motifs, though some of his last fabrics are too dependent on eighteenth century chinoiserie patterns.

Morris's own experiments with woven textiles had culminated in the magnificent *St James, Isphahan* and the sumptuous *Granada*, a woven silk velvet brocaded with gilt thread and costing £10 a yard. It is interesting however that *Brocatel* and *Golden Bough* have been attributed to both Morris and Dearle, for it was in the field of woven textiles especially that Dearle excelled.

He produced over thirty original designs. His early successful patterns were constructed on similar principles to his wallpapers, both *Vine* and *Golden Stem* being based on the strong, sinuous vertical, a motif seen at its best in the *Sunflower* of about 1890 where the use of white in contrast to shades of green is particularly effective.

Right: Daffodil. *This printed cotton was designed by Henry Dearle in c. 1891. While obviously reminiscent of Morris's manner, it also shows Dearle's own powers as a pattern designer.*

Opposite: *Dearle's magnificent* Compton *design dates from c. 1896 and was used as both a wallpaper and a textile. The outstanding quality of the pattern meant that it was long attributed to Morris himself.*

Like Morris, Dearle was also influenced by historic textiles. *Rose and Lily*, for example, was based on a seventeenth century Italian silk. Dearle's later designs show a greater feeling for colour range and texture, but, as with his printed fabrics, his final designs are too dependent on original sources. Indeed, Dearle was to supervise a number of reproduction fabrics woven by the Firm which proved popular in ecclesiastical circles.

Two magnificent carpets also date from Morris's later years. The earlier of these is the great *Clouds* carpet of 1887, woven for

the Wyndham family and originally laid in the house which gives the piece its name. This enormous carpet—thirty-nine feet long and over twelve feet wide—reveals the full power of Morris's skills in the field of carpet making. The border was taken from an earlier design, and its somewhat solid leaves are in excellent contrast to the fine pattern of pointed artichoke motifs that branch out from a centre to which they return with great ingenuity.

The second of these carpets is the *Bullerswood*, first woven in 1889 and twice repeated. This work is almost certainly a collaboration between Morris and Dearle. The long and sinuous branches that meander the length of the ground are close to Dearle's early chintz and wallpaper motifs, but the overall richness of effect and the subtle play of many colours are clearly close to Morris himself. The *Bullerswood* is a deeply satisfying work, but it was the last carpet in which Morris himself had any major involvement. Once again, Dearle was to develop this side of the Firm's work while Morris turned increasingly to tapestry.

This was a technique that stirred Morris deeply:

> The noblest of the weaving arts is tapestry: in which there is nothing mechanical: it may be looked upon as a mosaic of pieces of colour made up of dyed threads, and is capable of producing wall ornament of any degree of elaboration within the proper limits of duly considered decorative work. As in all wall-decoration, the first thing to be considered in the designing of tapestry is the force, purity and elegance of the silhouette of the object represented, and nothing vague or indeterminate is admissible. But special excellencies can be expected from it. Depth of tone, richness of colour, and exquisite gradation of tints are easily to be obtained in tapestry; and it also demands that crispness and abundance of beautiful detail which was the special characteristic of fully developed Medieval Art.

Despite these high ideals, the tapestries produced by Morris and the Firm are among the most problematic areas of their output.

Morris had achieved a considerable success with his early *Cabbage and Vine*, a *verdure* piece which reveals an understanding of the true nature of the medium. This is further explored in the *Woodpecker* of 1885, though the overall design is somewhat marred by the uneasy relationship between the excellent grey-green leaves swirling about the trunk of the tree and the tree itself with its simplistic suggestion of space filling. The borders of trailing honeysuckle have great charm however, while the embroidered inscriptions were to become a recurrent motif of the Firm's tapestry work.

Two other designs are also closely associated with Morris, though both are collaborative works. *The Orchard* adapts the angels painted on the roof of Jesus College chapel in 1866, making them into clearly female figures and placing them against a background designed by Dearle. Dearle himself later wrote of the piece that 'the colouring as well as the general design are by Mr Morris and parts of the figures have been woven by his own hands.' The result is a pleasing tapestry. The figures have volume while still preserving a two-dimensional emphasis, though only the figure on the extreme left is fully satisfactory in its articulation. The screen of trees and vines is a considerable achievement nonetheless, though the flowers in the foreground have perhaps too wooden a symmetry. As on the original chapel roof, the inscribed scroll provides a strong horizontal accent.

Morris insisted that the true tapestry maker '. . . must be able to draw well; he must be able to draw the human figure, especially hands and feet'. This was frequently a problem for Morris and is the reason why his contributions to *verdure* tapestry are conspicuously more successful than the rest of his work in the medium. His *Minstrel Figure*, for example, is feebly executed, the one appearing foot and hand being particularly poor, while the drapery gives no sense of a body beneath. The background by Dearle is more successful, though the foreground again reveals some of the shortcomings found in *The Orchard*.

These problems of collaborative tapestry design are revealed particularly clearly in a piece like *The Forest*. The acanthus ground of this work is by Morris and is the most successful element in the design. While Dearle contributed some of the foreground details, the animals derive from drawings by Philip Webb. With the exception of the magnificent peacock, which is a masterly piece of formal design and is excellently integrated into the ground, the rest of the animals are distinctly uncomfortable. The lion is merely weak, while the fox and the hare particularly have a realism which is wholly out of keeping with the other elements in the piece.

It was Burne-Jones who was to become the most important of Morris's collaborators in tapestry design, though the artistic limitations of some of his work in this field are akin to those in his later Morris windows: an effete mannerism and too great an emphasis on pictorial illusion.

The panels of *Flora* and *Pomona* on which Morris and Burne-Jones collaborated again show a relative lack of success in integrating the figures to the background, a problem somewhat more satisfactorily resolved by Dearle when he later experimented with *millefleur* designs for these areas.

The best known of the Firm's tapestries—those produced for churches or based on incidents from Malory—are only tenuously connected with Morris's own work as a designer. A number of these tapestries were adapted from Burne-Jones's cartoons for stained-glass windows and were given backgrounds designed by

Right: *The* Bullerswood *carpet.*

Below: *Morris's design for the* Redcar *carpet of c. 1881–85. It was such a design as this that would be shown to clients, and the colouring suggested here was actually used in the completed carpet.*

Left: *Morris's* Woodpecker *tapestry of 1885 is one of his first and most successful. It is clearly influenced by Flemish verdure pieces.*

now sit and see nor ride nor haste

Left: *The* Forest *tapestry of 1887 is a collaboration between Morris, Webb and Dearle. The acanthus leaves of the background show Morris's design at its best. Webb's peacock, too, is a fine achievement, though the lion is somewhat weak and the smaller animals verge on the realistic. Dearle contributed the design of plants in the foreground.*

Dearle. A particularly fine example of this collaboration is the *Angeli Laudantes*, based on a window in Salisbury cathedral. More popular however was the *Adoration* woven for Exeter College (where Morris and Burne-Jones were both Honorary Fellows) and subsequently repeated in at least ten versions. Despite Morris's excessive praise of the piece however, it cannot be considered as entirely successful. Its conception is far too close to easel painting, while the figures themselves are mannered, sentimental and focus on a Virgin of distinctly feeble design.

The *Holy Grail* series is altogether superior and ranks, indeed, as the most considerable experiment in all of nineteenth century tapestry weaving. These pieces were designed in 1890 for the dining room of Stanmore Hall, and the six figure panels were originally intended to hang at cornice level, while the *verdures* beneath them reached down to the skirting board.

A tapestry like 'The Arming and Departure of the Knights' is a truly magnificent piece with its figures excellently grouped without an excessive concern for anecdotal detail or illusionistic effect. The strong vertical accents of spears and swords, hair, manes and horses' tails complement the folds of the drapery to give a strong but never obtrusive surface pattern. Dearle's foreground flowers have little of the woodenness that so often vitiates his designs in this area, while the dark background forest again denies too illusionistic a sense of recession while providing an atmosphere of mystery just touched by the sinister.

Morris's contribution to the series was relatively slight, being chiefly restricted to the heraldic details. The vigorous abstract patterns he brought to his own *verdure* panels would have been inappropriate to what is essentially a narrative sequence, but in the panel representing the arms of the Knights of the Round Table he achieved a play of colour, a control of the heraldic and naturalistic, which is extremely successful.

Morris himself saw the *Holy Grail* cycle as a triumph of the apprenticeship offered by the Firm. Describing the first of the tapestries to be completed, he told an interviewer from *The Daily Chronicle*:

It occupied three persons, as many as can comfortably sit across the warp, for two years. The people who made it, and this is by far the most interesting thing about it, are boys, at least they're grown up by this time, entirely trained in our own shop. It is really free hand work, remember, not slavishly copying a pattern, like the 'haute lisse' method, and they come to us with no knowledge of drawing whatever, and have have learnt every single thing they know under our training. And most beautifully they have done it! I don't think you could want a better example than this of the value of apprenticeship.

That Morris should have used child labour is repellent to the modern liberal conscience, but the fact that he did so should be judged in terms of Victorian practice as well as by modern standards. In a period without compulsory formal education to the age of sixteen, children were important breadwinners for poorer families and, despite its serious limitations, an apprenticeship at the Merton Abbey works provided many boys with a training that later opened to them opportunities that would have been otherwise wholly beyond their reach. We should look first at the techniques they were required to follow.

Boys entering Merton Abbey were first employed in winding yarn onto bobbins for the weavers. After a number of trial attempts at weaving itself, they worked on background sections and apprentice pieces, moving on to larger figure designs that were often taken from cartoons for stained glass windows. Finally, the boys were permitted to work on commissioned pieces, first on areas of background and border and then progressing through more difficult sections until eventually being allowed to complete the flesh tones.

Morris himself preferred to hire such boy labourers because, he declared: 'The work of weaving is a kind which proves to be best done by boys. It involves little muscular effort and is best carried on by small flexible fingers.'

The boys themselves, who seem to have been about thirteen or fourteen, were lodged on site and were supervised by a housekeeper. Discipline was strict and appearances were maintained at all times by Morris's insistence that they wear black striped trousers and starched collars. Although the boys were permitted to wear a smock, this had to be removed when visitors came or photographs were being taken. In essence, this was a repetition of the standards set by a public school, and Morris himself tried to ensure:

> . . . that the workman shall take pleasure in his work, that decent conditions of light and breathing-space and cleanliness shall surround him, that he shall be made to feel himself not the brainless 'hand' but the intelligent cooperator, the *friend* of the man who directs his labour, that his honest toil shall inevitably win fair and comfortable wages, whatever be the low-water record of the market-price of men, that illness or trouble befalling him during his term of employment shall not mean dismissal or starvation.

The designs from which the boys worked originated in small sketches which were subsequently redrawn, coloured, resubmitted to the artist and corrected. The drawing was then photographed, enlarged to the envisaged size of the completed

Above: *The* Angeli Laudentes *tapestry.*

Right: *Burne-Jones's 'The Arming and the Departure of the Knights' from the* Holy Grail *series was first woven between 1890–94. In its sweet and hushed melancholy, its remote and dreamy world of idealism, it suggests the allure of the Arthurian tales recounted by Malory which both Morris and Burne-Jones had loved since their student days.*

tapestry and finished by adding the details of foreground and background on a tracing. A complete tracing of both the original and the details was then made and transferred to the warp threads on the loom by means of a small, sharp-edged piece of ivory dipped in ink. Trial colours were then woven on the edge of the warp, and only when approved by Morris or Dearle could the actual process of weaving begin.

The boys themselves were not paid for this preparation, which could take anything up to two days, but once they had begun the weaving itself they were remunerated at a rate of about £2 5s a square foot. Such an area would then retail at anything between twelve and sixteen guineas. Nor was such work entirely safe. Seated crouched before the looms, several of the boys developed stomach problems and in 1929 one actually died of a gastric ulcer.

If all this seems a long way from the ideals expressed in 'A Factory of the Future', a number of the apprentices profited greatly from their training. Dearle himself, of course, became the manager of the Merton Abbey works. Walter Taylor, who joined the Firm at the age of fourteen, became Head of the Weaving Department at the Central School of Arts and Crafts. John Martin became the first tapestry restorer to be employed by the Victoria and Albert Museum.

By the 1880s, Morris's fame as an interior decorator had become widespread. In his *Travels in South Kensington*, for example, Moncure Conway had described Bedford Park and told how 'The majority of residents have used wallpapers by William Morris . . . whose decorative work has become so serious that a branch of the . . . establishment will probably become necessary in the vicinity'. Contemporary novelists, playwrights and satirists also paid their due of praise, and while the English use of the Firm's products was largely focused in London as far as the middle classes were concerned, *The Daily Telegraph* reported that the wives of Oxford dons 'religiously clothed their walls in Norham Gardens and Bradmore Road with Morrissian designs of clustering pomegranates'.

The Firm also continued to decorate more splendid establishments, and even contributed to furnishing some of the first class cabins on the *Titanic*. Morris continued to inveigh against the general standard of taste among the wealthy, saying that he had never been in a rich man's house that would not have looked better for having nine-tenths of its contents burned. 'By this accumulation of useless things,' he declared, 'not only are beautiful things kept out, but the very sense of beauty is perpetually dulled and ground away.'

A few wealthy clients were people of finer discrimination. For example, Theodore Mander, the paint and varnish manufacturer, was greatly influenced by his reading of Ruskin when building his half-timbered Wightwick Manor in Staffordshire. Both the original house and its later extension have a quiet but sumptuous appeal that is dignified without being in the least overbearing. This is an effect greatly enhanced by the presence of Morris fabrics and papers which finely complement the dark, gleaming wood panelling which characterises much of the interior.

Two further houses, both of which were designed by Webb and furnished by Morris, show an important advance towards lightness of effect. The first of these was *Clouds* in Wiltshire, designed for the political and artistic circle centred around Percy Wyndham. The original impression made by this revolutionary and much praised house now has to be reconstructed from photographs, but what emerges is a feeling for lightness and space, for a 'great house' that does not seek to overwhelm. Victorian

Above: *Morris and Co were employed to decorate this luxury cabin on the* Titanic.

fussiness has been almost completely cleared and in its place are unstained woods, panels of white and the enriching colours of Morris fabrics. These included the specially woven *Clouds* carpet, *Peacock and Dragon* hangings and *Avon* and *Cray* furnishing fabrics. This scheme, paid for out of the £27, 000 insurance settlement made when the original house was burned down, was dispersed when the house was sold in 1933.

The second of these two late houses remains intact, however. *Standen* in East Sussex was a weekend retreat commissioned by a London solicitor. The interiors are light and pleasant, and a contemporary critic described how '. . . the human quality of the building lingers with one like a choice flavour'. The interior has a rather painstaking simplicity of effect nonetheless, and some of

Right: *The Great Parlour of Wightwick Manor.*

Below: *The drawing room at Standen.*

the detailing is austere to the point of being lifeless. The refined domesticity of these two houses made them buildings of considerable influence and they were important forerunners of the effects that were to be sought in smaller dwellings at the beginning of the twentieth century.

Morris's furnishing of his own homes and of Kelmscott House in particular shows the ambience in which he preferred to live. He declared of his London home that it '. . . could easily be done up at a cost of money, and might be made very beautiful with a touch of my art'.

The most impressive room in the house was the great drawing room, forty-four feet long and looking out over the river. This room Morris hung with the beautiful *Bird* woven fabric, a favourite design device which he had the greatest difficulty getting other people to accept. There was a blue carpet on the floor as well as some of Morris's other carpets, though the better items from his magnificent collection of oriental pieces were hung on the walls to protect them. Lustre plates on the fine fireplace (its grate designed by Webb) deepened the glowing richness of effect. Among the chief items of furniture were Webb's *Prioress* cabinet and a settle from Red Lion Square which were placed opposite each other. A large Webb table, covered with a carpet and more de Morgan pots, completed the scheme. Clearly, this was a masculine room of unaffected luxury decorated with items from a life of extraordinarily fecund productivity. There was also plenty of space in which to walk around, while the decoration was, in Mackail's words: '. . . a mass of subdued yet glowing colour into which the eye sank with a sort of active sense of rest.'

Morris's study, by contrast was, in his daughter's words: '. . . almost frugally bare; no carpets, and no curtains: his writing table in earlier times a plain deal board with trestles, the walls nearly lined with books; just a fine inlaid Italian cabinet in the corner.' Such simplicity was to have an increasing allure for Morris, and towards the end of his life he would enthuse about plain, whitewashed walls and simple wooden furniture enhancing 'some great room where one talked to one's friends in one corner, and ate in another, and slept in another, and worked in another'. It is an ideal of great attraction, suggesting as it does a balanced way of life in which work and friendship, public and private, have been brought together by a strong and integrated personality.

Indeed, Kelmscott House and its sage now attracted a wide range of the late nineteenth century intelligentsia. This was partly through Morris's generous decision to open the lectureroom in the stableblock to a range of Sunday speakers. Fabians such as Bernard Shaw and Sidney and Beatrice Webb were regular attenders, along with Annie Besant and Ernest Rhys. W. B. Yeats, then living in Bedford Park, met artists and craftsmen such as

Walter Crane and Emery Walker as well as such political figures as Hyndman and the anarchist Prince Kropotkin.

Morris's own socialist beliefs continued to be central to his vision of the world and, though his physical strength was beginning to diminish, he took part in the May Day rally of 1892. Three days later he was speaking beside Aveling, Engels, Shaw and Cunningham-Graham. In the autumn of that year publication of the *Hammersmith Socialist Review* began and Morris carried the banner of his society to meetings which he often addressed.

In 1893, a joint meeting of the Hammersmith Socialist Society, the Social Democratic Foundation and a number of leading Fabians tried to patch up a compromise. Its *Manifesto of English Socialists* declared: 'Our aim, one and all, is to obtain for the whole community complete ownership and control of the means of transport, the means of manufacture, the mines and the land. Thus we look to put an end for ever to the wage system, to sweep away all distinctions of class, and eventually to establish national and international Communism.'

Though Bernard Shaw did not believe in the usefulness of this alliance, Morris was still determined to see 'a due Socialist party established,' and he invited Keir Hardie of the Independent Labour Party to Hammersmith, realising that his own opposition to parliamentary activity had been misplaced. Morris was even invited to become leader of the party, an honour he declined, but he was now sufficiently reconciled with the Social Democratic Foundation to contribute to *Justice* one of his most moving autobiographical pieces: 'How I became a Socialist.' He also collaborated with Belfort Bax on *Socialism: Its Growth and Outcome* (1893) and in 1894 spoke in the Hyde Park May Day rally. Above all, Morris still believed passionately that: 'The first step . . . towards the new birth of art must be a definite rise in the condition of the workers.'

There was, nonetheless, some softening in his approach which the poet Wilfred Scawen Blunt (who had also suffered for his socialist convictions) attributed to disillusion. 'Morris was too loyal and obstinate to abjure his creed,' Blunt confided to his diary, 'but the heart of his devotion to the cause of the proletariat had gone. In some ways our two positions were the same. We had both of us sacrificed much socially to our principles, and our principles had failed to justify themselves by results, and we were both driven back on earlier loves, art, poetry, romance.'

These were themes that Morris was coming increasingly to embody in his prose fiction, works which contain some of his most precious as well as his most interesting writing.

In *A Tale of the House of the Wolfings* (1889), Morris adopted motifs from Icelandic literature—as well as developing the the artificial style of his own translations—to create a narrative in which he contrasts the commercial individualism of the Romans to the communal life of the Gothic tribe. In *The Roots of the Mountains* (1890), a longer and more diffuse work, Face-of-god develops from being 'one against the world' to a natural and successful leader of his people.

These Nordic elements are seen again in Morris's last volume of verse, *Poems by the Way*, published in 1891, where they are often combined with socialist themes. Indeed, the volume contains a number of Morris's songs written for the party, as well as translations from medieval Flemish, and such pieces of imagined history as 'The Folk-Mote by the River', a depiction of revolt against a feudal overlord in which Morris's ideals of benevolent nature and small, self-governing communities come to the fore. It was at this time too that a member of Gladstone's cabinet sounded out Morris as to whether he would accept the office of Poet Laureate. He naturally refused, being quite unprepared, in the words of *The Bookman*: '. . . to exchange lectures at Kelmscott House for songs about royal marriages.'

Morris continued instead with translations of medieval French romance, again offering these in a highly artificial, monosyllabic style which shows a distinct bias towards archaisms and Teutonic vocabulary. This is a style in direct opposition to the realism of the contemporary novel, just as the romances in which it was now employed—*The Wood Beyond the World* (1894), for instance—are similarly an escape into the spheres of imagination and symbolic action.

In *The Well at the World's End* (1896), perhaps the most satisfactory of these romances, the quest of the hero Ralph unites the themes of bravery, love and social responsibility, and ends with a satisfying feeling that maturity has been achieved. Such themes are seen again in *Child Christopher and Goldilind the Fair* (1895), *The Water of the Wondrous Isles* (posthumous 1897), and Morris's last romance *The Sundering Flood* (posthumous 1898). Such works make a deep appeal to those who enjoy the writings of such modern masters of fantasy as J.R. R. Tolkien.

Others of Morris's prose fictions, however, are more overt in their political content. *A Dream of John Ball* (1888), for example, belongs to the years of Morris's involvement with the Socialist League. This is a vision of England in 1381, the year of the Peasants' Revolt, and of the narrator's meeting with the priest and defeated rebel leader John Ball. It is a moving evocation of the intensely moral side of Morris's socialism, his belief in the dignity of struggle even when it is defeated, and of the fundamental value of community rather than communal strife.

It is in *News from Nowhere* (1891) however, that Morris achieved his most complete work of prose fiction. 'Nowhere', of course, translates the Greek word 'utopia', and the volume as a whole offers Morris's view of the fulfilment of mankind after the Socialist revolution. Written in part to contradict the image of a highly technological paradise portrayed in Edward Bellamy's *Looking Backward*, *News from Nowhere* presents a dream vision of equality, of man and woman living in harmony with each other and the aspirations of nature, and of a life where work has reassumed the delights of art.

He was a handsome young fellow, with a peculiarly pleasant and friendly look about his eyes,—an expression which was quite new to me then, though I soon became familiar with it. For the rest, he was dark-haired and berry-brown of skin, well-knit and strong, and obviously used to exercising his muscles, but with nothing rough or coarse about him, and clean as might be. His dress was not like any modern work-a-day clothes I had seen, but would have served very well as a costume for a picture of fourteenth-century life: it was of dark blue cloth, simple enough, but of fine web, and without a stain on it. He had a brown leather belt round his waist, and I noticed that its clasp was of damascened steel beautifully wrought. In short, he seemed to be like some specially manly and refined young gentleman, playing waterman for a spree, and I concluded that this was the case.

The characters in News from Nowhere *are irresistibly reminiscent of the hippies of the 1960s. Morris guessed that the socialist revolution would occur just a decade before this.*

And now again I was busy looking about me, for we were quite clear of Piccadilly Market, and were in a region of elegantly-built much ornamented houses, which I should have called villas if they had been ugly and pretentious, which was very far from being the case. Each house stood in a garden carefully cultivated, and running over with flowers. The blackbirds were singing their best amidst the garden-trees, which, except for a bay here and there, and occasional groups of limes, seemed to be all fruit trees: there were a great many cherry trees, now all laden with fruit, and several times as we passed by a garden we were offered baskets of fine fruit by children and young girls. Amidst all these gardens and houses it was of course impossible to trace the sites of the old streets, but it seemed to me that the main roadways were the same as of old.

We came presently into a large open space, sloping somewhat toward the south, the sunny site of which had been taken advantage of for planting an orchard, mainly, as I could see, of apricot trees, in the midst of which was a pretty gay little structure of wood, painted and gilded, that looked like a refreshment stall. From the southern side of the said orchard ran a long road, chequered over with the shadow of tall old pear

London after the Socialist revolution from News from Nowhere.

trees, at the end of which showed the high tower of the Parliament House, or Dung Market.

A strange sensation came over me; I shut my eyes to keep out the sight of the sun glittering on this fair abode of gardens, and for a moment there passed before them a phantasmagoria of another day. A great space surrounded by tall ugly houses, with an ugly church at the corner and a nondescript ugly cupolaed building at my back; the roadway thronged with a sweltering and excited crowd, dominated by omnibuses crowded with spectators. In the midst a paved be-fountained square, populated only by a few men dressed in blue, and a good many singularly ugly bronze images (one on top of a tall column). The said square guarded up to the edge of the roadway by a four-fold line of big men clad in blue, and across the southern roadway the helmets of a band of horse-soldiers, dead white in the greyness of the chilly November afternoon—

I opened my eyes to the sunlight again and looked round me, and cried out among the whispering trees and odorous blossoms, 'Trafalgar Square!'

One of the most interesting aspects of News from Nowhere *is Morris's keen analysis of the effects capitalism has on sexual relationships.*

Said I: 'That beautiful girl, is he going to be married to her?'

'Well,' said he, 'yes, he is. He has been married to her once already, and now I should say it is pretty clear that he will be married to her again.'

'Indeed,' quoth I, wondering what that meant.

'Here is the whole tale,' said old Hammond; 'a short one enough; and now I hope a happy one: they lived together two years the first time; were both very young; and then she got it into her head that she was in love with somebody else. So she left poor Dick; I say *poor* Dick, because he had not found any one else. But it did not last long, only about a year. Then she came to me, as she was in the habit of bringing her troubles to the old carle, and asked me how Dick was, and whether he was happy, and all the rest of it. So I saw how the land lay, and said that he was very unhappy, and not at all well; which last at any rate was a lie. There, you can guess the rest. Clara came to have a long talk with me to-day, but Dick will serve her turn much better. Indeed, if he hadn't chanced in upon me to-day I should have had to have sent for him to-morrow.'

'Dear me,' said I. 'Have they any children?'

'Yes,' said he, 'two; they are staying with one of my daughters at present, where, indeed, Clara has mostly been. I wouldn't lose sight of her, as I felt sure they would come together again: and Dick, who is the best of good fellows, really took the matter to heart. You see, he had no other love to run to, as she had. So I managed it all; as I have done with such-like matters before.'

'Ah,' said I, 'no doubt you wanted to keep them out of the Divorce Court: but I suppose it often has to settle such matters.'

Opposite: *The frontispiece to* News from Nowhere *is an illustration of Kelmscott Manor. In the novel the old house becomes the centre of a paradise created after the Socialist revolution.*

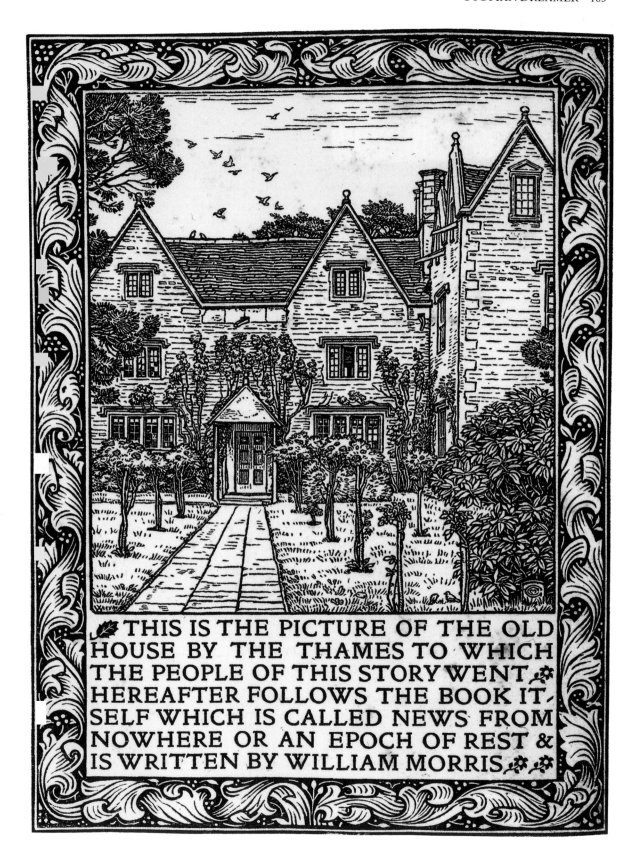

THIS IS THE PICTURE OF THE OLD HOUSE BY THE THAMES TO WHICH THE PEOPLE OF THIS STORY WENT. HEREAFTER FOLLOWS THE BOOK IT· SELF WHICH IS CALLED NEWS FROM NOWHERE OR AN EPOCH OF REST & IS WRITTEN BY WILLIAM MORRIS.

'Then you suppose nonsense,' said he. 'I know that there used to be such lunatic affairs as divorce courts. But just consider; all the cases that came into them were matters of property quarrels: and I think, dear guest,' said he, smiling, 'that though you do come from another planet, you can see from the mere outside look of our world that quarrels about private property could not go on amongst us in our days.'

Indeed, my drive from Hammersmith to Bloomsbury, and all the quiet happy life I had seen so many hints of, even apart from my shopping, would have been enough to tell me that 'the sacred rights of property,' as we used to think of them, were now no more. So I sat silent while the old man took up the thread of the discourse again, and said:

'Well, then, property quarrels being no longer possible, what remains in these matters that a court of law could deal with? Fancy a court for enforcing a contract of passion or sentiment! If such a thing were needed as a *reductio ad absurdum* of the enforcement of contract, such a folly would do that for us.'

He was silent again a little, and then said: 'You must understand once for all that we have changed these matters; or rather, that our way of looking at them has changed, as we have changed within the last two hundred years. We do not deceive ourselves, indeed, or believe that we can get rid of all the trouble that besets the dealings between the sexes. We know that we must face the unhappiness that comes of man and woman confusing the relations between natural passion, and sentiment, and the friendship which, when things go well, softens the awakening from passing illusions: but we are not so mad as to pile up degradation on that unhappiness by engaging in sordid squabbles about livelihood and position, and the power of tyrannising over the children who have been the result of love or lust.'

Again he paused awhile, and again went on: 'Calf love, mistaken for a heroism that shall be life-long, yet early waning into disappointment; the inexplicable desire that comes on a man of riper years to be the all-in-all to some one woman, whose ordinary human kindness and human beauty he has idealised into superhuman perfection, and made the one object of his desire; or lastly the reasonable longing of a strong and thoughtful man to become the most intimate friend of some beautiful and wise woman, the very type of the beauty and glory of the world which we love so well,—as we exult in all the pleasure and exaltation of spirit which goes with these things, so we set ourselves to bear the sorrow which not unseldom goes with them also.'

From Morris's views on the relation of capitalism to sexual relationships emerged an advanced feminist case.

'The men have no longer any opportunity of tyrannising over the women, or the women over the men; both of which things took place in those old times. The women do what they can do best, and what they like best, and the men are neither jealous of it or injured by it. This is such a commonplace that I am almost ashamed to state it.'

I said, 'O; and legislation? do they take any part in that?'

Hammond smiled and said: 'I think you may wait for an answer to that question till we get on to the subject of legislation. There may be novelties to you in that subject also.'

'Very well,' I said; 'but about this woman question? I saw at the Guest House that the women were waiting on the men: that seems a little like reaction, doesn't it?'

'Does it?' said the old man; 'perhaps you think housekeeping an unimportant occupation, not deserving of respect. I believe that was the opinion of the "advanced" women of the nineteenth century, and their male backers. If it is yours, I recommend to your notice an old Norwegian folk-lore tale called How the Man minded the House, or some such title; the result of which minding was that, after various tribulations, the man and the family cow balanced each other at the end of a rope, the man hanging half-way up the chimney, the cow dangling from the roof, which, after the fashion of the country, was of turf and sloping down low to the ground. Hard on the cow, *I* think. Of course no such mishap could happen to such a superior person as yourself,' he added, chuckling.

I sat somewhat uneasy under this dry gibe. Indeed, his manner of treating this latter part of the question seemed to me a little disrespectful.

'Come, now, my friend,' quoth he, 'don't you know that it is a great pleasure to a clever woman to manage a house skilfully, and to do it so that all the house-mates about her look pleased, and are grateful to her? And then, you know, everybody likes to be ordered about by a pretty woman: why, it is one of the pleasantest forms of flirtation. You are not so old that you cannot remember that. Why, I remember it well.'

And the old fellow chuckled again, and at last fairly burst out laughing.

'In your sense of the word, we have no criminal law either. Let us look at the matter closer, and see whence crimes of violence spring. By far the greater part of these in past days were the result of the laws of private property, which forbade the satisfaction of their natural desires to all but a privileged few, and of the general visible coercion which came of those laws. All *that* cause of violent crime is gone. Again, many violent acts came from the artificial perversion of the sexual passions, which caused overweening jealousy and the like miseries. Now, when you look carefully into these, you will find that what lay at the bottom of them was mostly the idea (a law-made idea) of the woman being the property of the man, whether he were husband,

Morris was keenly aware of the links between capitalism and crime as is shown by this passage from News from Nowhere.

father, brother, or what not. That idea has of course vanished with private property, as well as certain follies about the 'ruin' of women for following their natural desires in an illegal way, which of course was a convention caused by the laws of private property.

'Another cognate cause of crimes of violence was the family tyranny, which was the subject of so many novels and stories of the past, and which once more was the result of private property. Of course that is all ended, since families are held together by no bond of coercion, legal or social, but by mutual liking and affection, and everybody is free to come or go as he or she pleases. Furthermore, our standards of honour and public estimation are very different from the old ones; success in besting our neighbours is a road to renown now closed, let us hope for ever. Each man is free to exercise his special faculty to the utmost, and every one encourages him in so doing. So that we have got rid of the scowling envy, coupled by the poets with hatred, and surely with good reason; heaps of unhappiness and ill-blood were caused by it, which with irritable and passionate men—*i.e.*, energetic and active men—often led to violence.'

I laughed, and said: 'So that you now withdraw your admission, and say that there is no violence amongst you?'

'No,' said he, 'I withdraw nothing: as I told you, such things will happen. Hot blood will err sometimes. A man may strike another, and the stricken strike back again, and the result be a homicide, to put it at the worst. But what then? Shall we the neighbours make it worse still? Shall we think so poorly of each other as to suppose that the slain man calls on us to revenge him, when we *know* that if he had been maimed, he would, when in cold blood and able to weigh all the circumstances, have forgiven his maimer? Or will the death of the slayer bring the slain man to life again and cure the unhappiness his loss has caused?'

'Yes,' I said, 'but consider, must not the safety of society be safeguarded by some punishment?'

'There, neighbour!' said the old man, with some exultation. 'You have hit the mark. That *punishment* of which men used to talk so wisely and act so foolishly, what was it but the expression of their fear? And they had need to fear, since *they*—*i.e.*, the rulers of society—were dwelling like an armed band in a hostile country. But we who live amongst our friends need neither fear nor punish. Surely if we, in dread of an occasional rare homicide, an occasional rough blow, were solemnly and legally to commit homicide and violence, we could only be a society of ferocious cowards. Don't you think so, neighbour?'

Morris was keenly critical of state socialism, seeing it as an instrument of further social distress.

That machinery of life for the use of people who didn't know what they wanted of it, and which was known at the time as State Socialism, was partly put in motion, though in a very piecemeal way. But it did not work smoothly; it was, of course, resisted at every turn by the capitalists; and no wonder, for it tended more and more to upset the commercial system I have told you of, without providing anything really effective in its place. The result was growing confusion, great suffering amongst the working classes, and, as a consequence, great discontent. For a long time matters went on like this. The power of the upper classes had lessened, as their command over wealth lessened, and they could not carry things wholly by the high hand as they had been used to in earlier days. So far the State Socialists were justified by the result. On the other hand, the working classes were ill-organised, and growing poorer in reality, in spite of the gains (also real in the long run) which they had forced from the masters. Thus matters hung in the balance, the masters could not reduce their slaves to complete subjection, though they put down some feeble and partial riots easily enough. The workers forced their masters to grant them ameliorations, real or imaginary, of their condition, but could not force freedom from them. At last came a great crash.

'Books, books! always books, grandfather! When will you understand that after all it is the world we live in which interests us; the world of which we are a part, and which we can never love too much? Look!' she said, throwing open the casement wider and showing us the white light sparkling between the black shadows of the moonlit garden, through which ran a little shiver of the summer night-wind, 'look! these are our books in these days!—and these,' she said, stepping lightly up to the two lovers and laying a hand on each of their shoulders; 'and the guest there, with his oversea knowledge and experience;—yes, and even you, grandfather' (a smile ran over her face as she spoke), 'with all your grumbling and wishing yourself back again in the good old days,—in which, as far as I can make out, a harmless and lazy old man like you would either have pretty nearly starved, or have had to pay soldiers and people to take the folk's victuals and clothes and houses away from them by force. Yes, these are our books; and if we want more, can we not find work to do in the beautiful buildings that we raise up all over the country (and I know there was nothing like them in past times), wherein a man can put forth whatever is in him, and make his hands set forth his mind and his soul.'

She paused a little, and I for my part could not help staring at her, and thinking that if she were a book, the pictures in it were most lovely. The colour mantled in her delicate sunburnt cheeks; her grey eyes, light amidst the tan of her face, kindly looked on us all as she spoke. She paused, and said again:

'As for your books, they were well enough for times when intelligent people had but little else in which they could take pleasure, and when they must needs supplement the sordid

In News from Nowhere *the aftermath of the Socialist revolution gives men and women a rapt appreciation of nature and a degree of contempt for book learning.*

miseries of their own lives with imaginations of the lives of other people. But I say flatly that in spite of all their cleverness and vigour, and capacity for story-telling, there is something loathsome about them. Some of them, indeed, do here and there show some feeling for those whom the history-books call "poor," and the misery of whose lives we have some inkling; but presently they give it up, and towards the end of the story we must be contented to see the hero and heroine living happily in an island of bliss on other people's troubles; and that after a long series of sham troubles (or mostly sham) of their own making, illustrated by dreary introspective nonsense about their feelings and aspirations, and all the rest of it; while the world must even then have gone on its way, and dug and sewed and baked and built and carpentered round about these useless—animals.'

'There!' said the old man, reverting to his dry sulky manner again. 'There's eloquence! I suppose you like it?'

'Yes,' said I, very emphatically.

By presenting himself as a visitor in this dream of the future, Morris can convey both his wonder and delight at a world free of pollution and commercial warfare. Friendship and natural relationships, a variety of delightful work and an easy rapport between town and country living, all create an ideal world. Children are educated naturally rather than through the forcing of scholarship and so acquire such skills and knowledge as may be truly useful to them. Prisons have been abolished in a world where common ownership means that there can be no crime against property. Factories are no longer sweatshops where men and women work in an alienated purgatory, but are places of delight and true creativity. Sexual relations are free, unforced by the constraints of marriage and the compulsion to social domination by men. As a result, women are no longer chattels in a world ruled by money alone.

Central government has also gone (the Houses of Parliament are now used to store manure) and people reach decisions in small communal assemblies. In the chapter entitled 'How the Change Came', Morris offers a fully Marxist interpretation of this process which accepts the need for revolution to overturn the old order. Much of this section develops Morris's experience of 'Bloody Sunday', though in his fiction at least Morris could develop his view of the class struggle so that we see the mounting pressure on the capitalists forced by labour and the withering of State socialism through the power of the strike weapon. The final result is 'an epoch of rest', a world where small is beautiful, where communism has led to the rural commune, where nature is respected and men and women enjoy freedom from the horrors once forced on them by alienated labour.

In its way, *News from Nowhere* is a remarkably prescient volume. While much of it prefigures the world of the 1960s (it is actually set a decade earlier) it also raises questions that remain challenging. The book is, for example a vivid antidote to the obvious waste and squalor of much capitalism as well as an exploration of both love of man and of nature. If *News from Nowhere* remains a vision that accepts perhaps too sentimentally the possibility of attaining human perfection, it is nonetheless a very fully imagined riposte to the Victorian values in which Morris himself was enmeshed.

The writing of such works stimulated Morris's interest in printing. In November 1888, Emery Walker, who lived near Morris in Hammersmith, delivered a lecture on typography, illustrating his talk with enlarged photographs of typefaces. The following month, the Chiswick Press printed Morris's *The House of the Wolfings* in a modified sixteenth century type. This was not altogether satisfactory in terms of spacing, and the following year Morris issued *The Roots of the Mountains*, using a slightly modified version of the same Chiswick fount. From now on, Morris was to assert that: 'To enjoy good houses and good books in self-respect and decent comfort, seems to me the pleasurable end towards which all societies of human beings ought now to struggle.' Such a belief was to be the spur to Morris's last great essay in the crafts: the founding of the Kelmscott Press.

In his posthumously published *Notes by William Morris on His Aims in Founding the Kelmscott Press*, Morris declared:

I began printing books with the hope of producing some which would have a definite claim to beauty, while at the same time they should be easy to read and should not dazzle the eye, or trouble the intellect of the reader by eccentricity of form in the letters. I have always been a great admirer of the calligraphy of the Middle Ages, of the earlier printing which took its place. As to fifteenth-century books, I had noticed that they were always beautiful by force of the mere typography, even without the added ornament, with which many of them are so lavishly supplied. And it was the essence of my undertaking to produce books which it would be a pleasure to look upon as pieces of printing and arrangement of type. Looking at my adventure from this point of view, then, I found I had to consider chiefly the following things: the paper, the form of the type, the relative spacing of the letters, the words and the lines; and lastly the position of the printed matter on the page.

Morris sought typographical beauty in what was 'architecturally good'. By this he meant clarity and ease of reading which in turn derived from well-formed letters and duly proportioned margins. He sought a balance of design across the recto (right side) and verso (left side) of an opening. He also insisted that spacing should not be excessive (too much white tends to dazzle the eye) and that the whole should be knit together like good brickwork. Typically, with his concern for quality, he also insisted on the highest standards of presswork and the best materials. Hand-made linen paper was specially prepared and ink was imported from Hanover.

In designing his own typefaces, Morris looked first to the Venetian printers of the late fifteenth century. Reacting against both the beautiful Aldine types (which he found too spindly) and what he condemned as the 'sweltering hideousness' of eighteenth century faces, Morris's Golden type is derived from founts used by Nicholas Jensen and Jacques le Rouge, both of which are more solid than those which Morris rejected. The design of the Golden type took him a year. When this was completed, he went on to produce two versions of a Gothic type, calling the larger Troy and the smaller Chaucer. Here his aim was to '. . . redeem the Gothic character from the charge of unreadableness which is commonly brought against it'.

Morris involved himself deeply in learning the techniques of printing, talking to and watching the work of compositors at every stage in the production of the printed sheet. The actual work of the Kelmscott Press was nonetheless left to experienced printers. Further, while his press itself was in many ways similar to that used by Caxton, Morris did not eschew modern techniques when he saw that nothing would be lost by them. All three of his typefaces, for example, were machine cut, while Burne-Jones's pencil illustrations were redrawn in ink and then transferred by photography onto the woodblocks from which they were printed. Morris designed the borders and the initials, and when these were repeatedly used they were printed from electrotypes.

The Kelmscott Press was originally established at 16 Upper Mall, close to Morris's London home, though it soon moved into larger premises in the neighbouring Sussex Cottage. By 2 March 1891, the first sheet of *The Glittering Plain* had been printed off, and although this book was originally intended only for circulation among a few of Morris's friends, news of the enterprise got out and, somewhat to his annoyance and concern over quality, a further one hundred and eighty copies had to be printed. These rapidly sold out, despite the fact that paper copies were printed at two guineas, while those produced on vellum barely covered their production cost at fifteen guineas each. The Kelmscott Press was thus in no sense a popular concern. Its fifty-three titles and total output of 18,234 volumes invariably appealed to collectors, many of whom had a speculative interest in their purchases.

As Morris's biographer Philip Henderson has written: 'The effect of brilliancy in the Kelmscott books is achieved by the thick and very black letters on the white page, reinforced by initials and foliage of white upon a dark background.' Decorative woodcuts or the use of coloured inks helps to lighten this effect as does the comparatively small amount of type on each page of the press's volumes of poetry.

While many of these smaller volumes are delightful, the major achievement of the Kelmscott Press was its edition of Chaucer. Morris began designing the ornaments for this in 1893 while he was working on his translation of *Beowulf* (the least satisfactory of his literary works) and Burne-Jones was working on the designs for the woodblocks. Work proceeded slowly, and printing only began on 8 August 1894. Four hundred and twenty-five copies of the Chaucer were printed and the volume was readily subscribed.

The Kelmscott Chaucer is one of the greatest English books, indeed one of the great books of the world. Its physical presence is exceptionally powerful and refined. The white pig skin binding with its silver clasps was executed by Cobden-Sanderson's bindery by Douglas Cockerell after a design by Morris himself, and it produces an initial impression of great solemnity. When opened, the effect is of extraordinary richness.

The Kelmscott Chaucer is not simply a text to be read however, but a deeply involving aesthetic experience in which the eye and the mind are constantly delighted by the poetry and its typographical layout, by the pages of black-letter press, by the beautifully decorated initials, by the intricate patterns of the borders, and the pleasingly graceful Pre-Raphaelite visions offered by Burne-Jones's eighty-seven illustrations.

The Chaucer is the last and greatest collaboration between two lifelong friends and draws on far more than their technical expertise. Here is the dream of the Middle Ages that had always sustained them now brought to its apogee, a medieval world without the profound spiritual involvement and vivifying bawdy of the Middle Ages and so in the last analysis essentially a Victorian solace: a world of sumptuous yet escapist craftsmanship, of rich aesthetic satisfaction sustained by nature and a love of the past.

In addition to making beautiful books, Morris was also buying them. His collection of medieval illuminated and early printed books was one of the great delights of his old age, and it was a pleasure on which he was prepared to spend a great deal of money. An English Book of Hours from about 1300 cost upwards of £400. Morris also owned the Huntingfield Psalter and

Incipit secunda pars

AMONGES thise povre folk ther dwelte a man
Which that was holden povrest of hem alle;
But hye God som tyme senden kan
His grace into a litel oxes stalle:
Janicula men of that throop hym calle.
A doghter hadde he, fair ynogh to sighte,
And Grisildis this yonge mayden highte.

But for to speke of vertuous beautee,
Thanne was she oon the faireste under sonne;
For povreliche yfostred up was she,
No likerous lust was thurgh hire herte yronne;
Wel ofter of the welle than of the tonne
She drank, and for she wolde vertu plese,
She knew wel labour, but noon ydel ese.

But thogh this mayde tendre were of age,
Yet in the brest of hire virginitee
Ther was enclosed rype and sad corage,
And in greet reverence and charitee
Hir olde povre fader fostred shee;
A fewe sheep, spynnynge, on feeld she kepte,
She wolde noght been ydel til she slepte.

And whan she homward cam, she wolde brynge
Wortes, or other herbes, tymes ofte,

FER FRO THILKE PALAYS HONUR-
ABLE
Theras this markys shoop his mariage,
Ther stood a throop, of site delitable,
In which that povre folk of that village
Hadden hir beestes and hir herbergage,
And of hire labour tooke hir sustenance,
After that the erthe yaf hem habundance.

the Tiptoft Missal, as well as a number of works by early German printers.

Morris would also spend time and money helping those anarchists of the Socialist League who fell foul of the law. This was particularly generous in view of his opinion of such people, but when the publisher of the *Commonweal* was brought before the courts for denouncing the judges who had condemned some bombers, Morris stood surety for £500 so that the man could attend his wife's funeral.

Morris continued his work as a translator while, having secured his lease on Kelmscott Manor, he also began carefully restoring the building by removing machine-made tiles

Above: *Morris's library in Kelmscott House. It was here that he kept his immensely valuable collection of medieval manuscripts.*

Opposite: The Clerk's Tale *from the Kelmscott Chaucer.*

and revitalising stone flags that had been hidden under floorboards.

He also continued to work hard for the Society for the Protection of Ancient Buildings, campaigning against proposed restorations to Peterborough Cathedral and Westminster Abbey, battling with the Thames Conservancy Board, a body which often raised his temper and showed the bluntness of his Anglo-Saxon language. Morris's letter to the *Daily Chronicle* newspaper about tree felling in Epping Forest was also written at this time and is a particularly fine example of the vigour of his campaign style.

Morris on tree felling in Epping Forest from the Daily Chronicle, *1895.*

We are told that a committee of 'experts' has been formed to sit in judgement on Epping Forest: but, Sir, I decline to be gagged by the word 'expert', and I call on the public generally to take the same position. An 'expert' may be a very dangerous person, because he is likely to narrow his views to the particular business (usually a commercial one) which he represents. In this case, for instance, we do not want to be under the thumb of either a wood bailiff, whose business is to grow timber for the market, or of a botanist whose business is to collect specimens for a botanical garden; or of a landscape gardener whose business is to vulgarize a garden or landscape to the utmost extent that his patron's purse will allow of. What we want is reasonable men of real artistic taste to take into consideration what the essential needs of the case are, and to advise accordingly.

It was clear however that Morris's energies were now running down. Diabetes and a few minor complications were diagnosed, though at first there was not thought to be any immediate danger. Nonetheless, at the opening of 1889, Morris gave what was to be the last of his Sunday lectures at Kelmscott House, and at the end of January spoke for the last time in public, seconding a motion of a society devoted to 'checking the Abuses of Public Advertising' which declared that: 'It is a national interest to protect rural scenery from unnecessary disfigurement and to maintain dignity and propriety in the aspect of our times'.

Morris's physical deterioration was now becoming evident to his friends. 'The ground beneath one is shifting, and I travel among quicksands,' Burne-Jones wrote. Other friends too noticed the decline, though Morris was still talking as energetically as ever. The work of restorers in particular continued to rouse his fury. 'Beasts! Pigs! Damn their souls!' he roared at the work done to the Norman tower at Shipley.

Finally his doctor Sir William Broadbent suggested a cruise to Norway. Morris had been talking much about his earlier trips to Iceland and he had, recorded Scawen Blunt: 'a sick man's fancy to go there again.' The trip, nonetheless, was not a success. Morris was restless, weary and depressed. He was too weak to make any inland excursions and he began to suffer from hallucinations. Coils of rope lying on the deck '. . . appeared to his disordered mind like a great serpent preparing to crush the life out of him'. He was more cheerful on the return journey, but arriving in London he found himself too weak to make the journey to Kelmscott Manor. Congestion of the left lung set in and with it general organic deterioration.

It was clear that Morris was now dying. Cobden-Sanderson recorded how he 'sits speechless waiting for the end to come'. On 3 October 1896 Morris died, aged just sixty-two. One of his doctors declared that the cause of his death was 'simply being William Morris and having done more work than most ten men.'

Morris was buried in Kelmscott churchyard three days later. Although most of his socialist colleagues stayed away for fear of offending Jane, it was otherwise a funeral such as Morris himself might have wished. It was a day of autumn storms and running water. At Lechlade station, the coffin was met by a red and yellow farm waggon wreathed in vine, willow and bulrushes. It was attended by four countrymen in moleskin clothes. After the service in the church which had been decorated for harvest festival, the plain coffin of unpolished oak with its wrought iron handles was buried beneath a long, coped gravestone shaped like a roof and designed by Webb after a traditional pattern. It was a tribute perfectly in keeping with much that Morris had stood for: integrity of life beautified by art and drawing its sustenance from the spirit of the past and the beauty of the English landscape.

THE INHERITORS

During the 1880s and '90s, the influence of Morris's ideas on design became increasingly apparent. A new public, interested in how their world could be fashioned, aware of earlier failings and responsive to Morris's concern with truth to materials and sound design, was ever more ready to build and decorate their houses after his manner. In addition, and influenced more by Morris's writings perhaps than by his actual products, a number of young men were developing an interest in the crafts and in what Sir Nikolaus Pevsner has called 'the organic inter-relationship between material, working process, purpose and aesthetic form.' As they began to work and talk together, so these people gradually evolved what, in 1888, Cobden-Sanderson was to call the 'Arts and Crafts' movement.

The inspiration of Morris was seminal here, though Morris, with his profound commitment to the Socialist cause, was often sceptical of a change in design that was not accompanied by an equally radical concern with changing society. Nonetheless, as May Morris declared: 'The busy and fruitful years of the eighties [saw] my Father in the association with men, many of them younger than himself, who felt that the time had come to proclaim the importance of the arts to modern life, and to that end to group themselves into a body that could meet and discuss and find ways to forward the cause of Art.' A number of associations were to emerge from this. The Century Guild, the Art Workers' Guild and the Arts and Crafts Exhibition Society were based in London. C. R. Ashbee, a Morrissian socialist inspired by the ideal of the simple and communal rural life advocated in *News from Nowhere*, set up workshops run by committees of workmen in Gloucestershire, while in 1903 Ernest Gimson and Sidney Barnsley set up their Cotswold School in nearby Sapperton. Each of these was to help develop Morris's concern with a better and more beautiful life for ordinary people. Each to some degree reflected his preference for small, cooperative groups. All of them had an important influence in furthering his ideas.

Opposite: Crown Imperial *was designed by Lindsay Butterfield in c. 1893 and printed by Thomas Wardle. The influence of Morris is clearly evident in this piece, but a more austere geometric emphasis stresses the formal qualities of the design.*

We should welcome even the feeble protest which is now being made against the vulgarization of all life: first because it is one token amongst others of the sickness of modern civilization; and next, because it may help to keep alive memories of the past which are necessary elements of the life of the future and methods of work which no society could afford to lose. In short, it may be said that though the movement towards the revival of handicraft is contemptible on the surface in face of the gigantic fabric of commercialism; yet taken in connection with the general movement towards freedom of life for all, on which we are now surely embarked, as a protest against intellectual tyranny, and a token of the change which is transforming civilization into socialism, it is both noteworthy and encouraging.

The three chief figures in the Century Guild were Herbert Horne, Selwyn Image and the most dominant of these men, Arthur H. Mackmurdo.

The Prospectus Mackmurdo issued clearly shows his debt to Morris. The aim of the Century Guild was, he declared:

> . . . to render all branches of Art, the sphere, no longer of tradesmen, but of the artist. It would restore building, decorating, glass-painting, pottery, wood-carving and metal-work to their rightful place beside painting and sculpture. By so placing them they would once more be regarded as legitimate and honoured expressions of the artistic spirit, and would stand in their true relation not only to sculpture and painting but to the drama, to music, and to literature. In other words, the Century Guild seeks to emphasise *Unity of Art*; and by thus dignifying Art in all its forms it hopes to make it living, a thing of our own century, and of the people.

This clearly reflects ideas that had preoccupied Morris since the founding of the Firm and which had been given expression in such lectures as 'The Lesser Arts'. While Morris however had been designer, craftsman and businessman—and had further gone on to give his vision a well thought out political basis—Mackmurdo differed from him on a number of points. He was chary of Morris's socialism, for example, while the Guild itself was essentially a collection of designers displaying their work in the showrooms at 28 Southampton Street which also served as a centre for the distribution of information about the craftsmen attracted to it. These included such interior designers as Agnes and Rhoda Garret, makers of wrought iron and chased brass, tile painters, sculptors and glass workers.

Mackmurdo also realised that if good design were to become popular it could only do so through the use of the machine. This was a difficult decision for him to reach, but he was eventually to declare: 'Great and unimaginable things may in the future result from a more true marriage between art and industry, where hitherto it has been but an ephemeral and promiscuous union.' His hope was to make the world less sordid for more people, and through the Century Guild itself to create an '. . . unbroken sentiment and strength of individuality guaranteed by a guild of fellow-craftsmen'.

Like Morris, Mackmurdo was convinced that designers should create a total ambience in which a client lived, an environment that was integrated, simpler and lighter than the conventional houses and furnishings of the period. His aim, in the words of Peter Stansky, was to create '. . . objects for a new sort of individual, more concerned with what would be the design of the world, and less anxious, through the ostentation of surroundings, to indicate status. They were designed for a society that was beginning to be more reflective about itself'.

This can be seen in the building of houses that aimed at a natural and traditional quality which enhanced the life of their inhabitants. In the words of C. F. A. Voysey, one of the greatest English domestic architects of this period, though a man who in his independence vehemently denied allegiance to the Arts and Crafts movement: 'Simplicity, sincerity, repose, directness and frankness are moral qualities as essential to good architecture as to good men.' Indeed, it was hoped that the one would create the other.

This moral aim was furthered by stripping out purely decorative elements and reusing traditional motifs in a simplified manner that became a first step on the road to modernism. Norman Shaw and the English Domestic Revival Movement gave a new dignity to the English vernacular by building houses in which the elements of construction were clear rather than artfully hidden. In Voysey's own house, The Orchard at Chorley Wood, a feeling of solidity and protection is gained by the use of a heavy roof, thick sloping walls, by the employment of traditional materials and the deliberately understated allegiance to seventeenth-century rural architecture. Voysey's unexecuted designs for two cottages again show these qualities of stylish traditionalism

Such feelings were even more in evidence in the interiors of Arts and Crafts houses. The fireplace of the main room, often an inglenook, was given elaborate treatment to stress the idea of hearth and home. A feeling of integrity was furthered by a handcrafted appearance: the use of beams and stone, woods and wools, furniture that revealed its construction rather than hid it behind elaborate ornament. These were feelings reinforced by the use of animals and plant forms as decorative motifs. Intimacy, tradition, light and homeliness sustained by natural and domestic values became all important to the Arts and Crafts house. The moral and aesthetic qualities aimed at by Morris in his decorative schemes are here given popular expression.

Domestic buildings such as Mackmurdo's Brooklyn house also reflect this purity of conception, as does his interest in traditional values of workmanship, but it is in Mackmurdo's use of the whip-line curve that he can be seen at his most distinctive. This is revealed by two works that importantly suggest the rise of art nouveau, though Mackmurdo himself would have denied this. The back of the chair Mackmurdo designed in the early 1880s, for example, has great elegance and richness of silhouette, while his title page for his book on Wren's City churches with its dramatic, swirling rhythms and vibrant use of black and white, is a landmark of English two dimensional design.

Right: *Chair by A. H. Mackmurdo.*

Indeed, innovation in typographical design was one of the most important areas of the work of the Century Guild, and was of considerable influence on Morris. Nowhere is this concern with typography clearer than in the Century Guild's *Hobby Horse*, the group journal, in which Emery Walker was also much involved.

The *Hobby Horse* was, in Herbert Horne's words: '. . . a quiet garden of literature, kept free from argument 'for the setting forth of high principles''.' While not over-distinguished in content, the design principles of unity between type, illustration and the disposition of these on the page, was of great influence, as was the magazine's famous cover of 1884 designed by Selwyn Image. The magazine was a work of art, and though its circulation was restricted to about 500, its concept was profoundly influential.

Horne played a decisive part in this—he was the main editor of the journal—and he was also an architect and designer of some distinction. His wallpapers and textiles are amongst the most interesting of the Century Guild, as can be seen in his delightful *Angel with Trumpet* cretonne and his *Bay Leaf* wallpaper, which was printed from woodblocks by Jeffrey and Co. Indeed, firms like Jeffrey's and retailers like Liberty played a vital role in encouraging the design of wallpaper and fabrics from such major figures as Voysey, Walter Crane, Lindsay Butterfield and Lewis F. Day. Designers were now becoming household names, and the Silver Studio was responsible, among other things, for adapting Morris designs for machine production and thereby extending their popularity.

The quality of many of these designs is exceptional and reveals the liberating influence that Morris had on his contemporaries. Slavish imitation is far from evident here. There is experimentation based on Morris's ideals rather than necessarily on his own motifs. *Angel and Trumpet*, for example, has a lightness and exultation which works magnificently as both a furnishing fabric and when hung in pleats. The *Bay Leaf* shows an excellent control of formal qualities, while being nonetheless a rather dominating design. Walter Crane, who was often influenced by Morris's earliest wallpapers—*Daisy* in particular—also revealed in *Rose Bush* a delicacy of colour which is exceptional. Fabrics by the Silver Studio sometimes show a free use of Morrissian motifs which are lighter than those of Morris himself, and this is achieved partly by a greater emphasis on formalism than Morris usually allowed himself.

It is Voysey however who showed himself as the most adept exponent of these new directions in design. There is a freshness, a pure and simple sense of joy about Voysey's best papers and fabrics which was widely appreciated at the time. Historical precedent and even the example of Morris have been absorbed into

Below: *Mackmurdo's title page to* Wren's City Churches *is an early and brilliant example of* art nouveau.

something altogether fresher, a desire to 'live and work in the present', as Voysey expressed the matter. 'It was,' wrote a contemporary, 'as if Spring had come all of a sudden.'

WREN'S CITY CHURCHES

BY
A·H·MACKMURDO, A·R·I·B·A,
1883
G.ALLEN, SUNNYSIDE, ORPINGTON, KENT.

Right: *Herbert Horne's* Angel with Trumpet *fabric of 1884.*

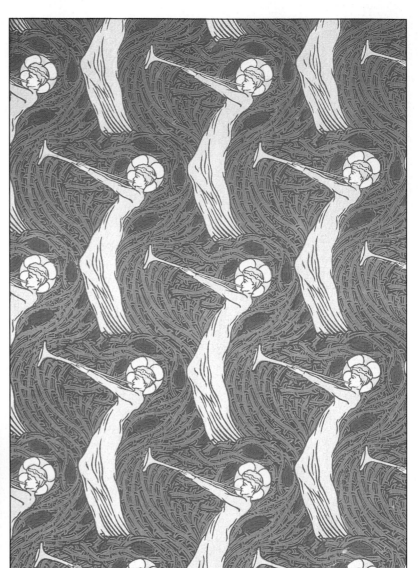

Below: *A detail of the Crown Imperial fabric by Lindsay Butterfield c. 1893.*

Right: Bay Leaf *by Herbert Horne, designed in c. 1882. Horne was Mackmurdo's pupil, and this wallpaper suggests the Century Guild's ideal of rendering 'all branches of art no longer the sphere of the tradesman but of the artist.'*

Opposite: Rose Bush, *designed by Walter Crane, was exhibited in the 1900 Paris international exhibition. This block-printed wallpaper is at once delicate but luxurious.*

The second of the Arts and Crafts groups founded in the 1880s was the Art Workers' Guild. This organisation was again dedicated to breaking down the barriers of class and creativity between makers and designers, and the Guild still recognises the importance of Morris by placing his bust over the Master's chair in its Meeting Room.

Morris's first biographer J.W. Mackail on the aims of the Arts and Crafts Movement.

On the one hand it aimed at a new organization of work within the single workshop, so that the manager, the designer, and the artificer should cease to be three distinct persons belonging to different social grades, differently educated and differently employed, working without mutual sympathy, or even each in active hostility to the others. On the other hand it expressed itself to the coordination of these workshops, hitherto isolated units of productive energy, whether by means of formal guilds and associations, or through more intangible links of common ideas and kindred enthusiasms, into the beginnings of a trained organism of handicraftsmen, with a mutual intercommunication, and a cumulative force of trained intelligence. What Morris himself had, in earlier days done by the mere unassisted force of his own genius, was now being attempted on all sides with a conscious purpose.

The Art Workers' Guild emerged from the combination of a group of young architects such as W. R. Lethaby (men much influenced by Webb), who felt 'separated from the craftsman by the business of trade', and the Committee of Fifteen, a group of decorative artists centred around Walter Crane, who were equally dissatisfied with the exclusivity of the Royal Academy. The ideal of breaking down such barriers was central to the thinking of both Ruskin and Morris, and the Art Worker's Guild existed to give such modern idealists a sense of cohesion and social role. Though Morris accepted the Presidency, he again questioned the limitations of such an essentially middle class group. 'An intellectual revolt had sprung up against the degradation of the arts,' he declared, stating that it had 'achieved the temporary and outward successes on a limited scale'. He warned, nonetheless: 'I hinted to you that this revolt carried on these lines could never be lastingly or widely successful because it was an intellectual revolt only and expressed the hopes and fears of a small body of men only.'

Such pessimism was not altogether justified, since Lethaby was to be a figure of some influence. He was fully at one with Ruskin and Morris on the relation of labour to art, for example, declaring: 'Art is best thought of as fine and sound ordinary work. So understood it is the widest, best, and most necessary form of culture.' He added that: 'Life is best thought of as service: service is common productive work; labour may be turned into joy by thinking of it as art, art, thought of as fine ordinary work, is the widest and best form of culture.' There is something of the austerity of Webb's socialism here—by which Lethaby was much influenced—and he put his ideals into practice partly through his educational work.

Where, in the words of Quentin Bell, the purpose of the early Victorian Design Schools, riddled as they were by the constraints of class, '. . . was emphatically not to produce artists but rather to form the taste of artisans,' when Lethaby became co-principal of the Central School of Design, Morris's ideas were placed in a formal educational context. The value of a widely available craft training came to be recognised, a development further symbolised when in 1901 Lethaby became Professor of Design at the Royal College of Art.

Walter Crane, whose political ideals are suggested by his design *Labour's May Day* symbolising 'Solidarity of Labour' under the goddess of Freedom, was also an eminent teacher. He was, for example, director of design at the Manchester Municipal School of Art and, for an unhappy year, principal of the Royal College of Art. His aim was to teach '. . . design in concrete forms, and in direct relation to tools, methods and materials, with the object of calling out the individual feeling and setting it free to express itself under the natural limitations of art in its own way'. Like Morris, Crane believed passionately in the values of the art of the Middle Ages, and in one of his many influential publications, *The Relations of Art to Education and Social Life*, he implicitly compared these to the ideals of the Arts and Crafts Movement: 'In that period we see the evolution of free and beautiful art perfectly expressive and organic, because perfectly adapted to the wants of the time, whether ecclesiastical, civil, military or domestic: an art, too, entirely unencumbered with pedantry.'

Crane wrote of the Art Workers' Guild that it was a true fellowship of the arts, 'men of all crafts meeting on common ground'. It grew rapidly from fifty members in 1884 to one hundred and eighty-two members just over ten years later. These people included painters, architects, sculptors, designers, metalworkers, weavers, dyers, wood-engravers, goldsmiths and bronze founders. The craft ideal was central to them all, but while they opposed the formal exclusivity of both the Royal Academy and the Institute of Architects, they were not an openly radical group. The Art Workers' Guild was essentially a forum for discussion and for promoting among its members ideas of design that veered away from Victorian complexity towards a more modern style.

If the Art Workers' Guild was primarily dedicated to the exchange of ideas, the Arts and Crafts Exhibition Society was organised to display to the public the work of craftsmen opposed to the exclusivity of the Royal Academy and the poverty of much official modern design. Morris had written vehemently against the current standards of the Academy, while Crane had also campaigned against it. It was probably W. A. S Benson however, a distinguished metalwork designer, who had the idea of the exhibition itself.

Morris was profoundly scathing of the official art exhibited at the Royal Academy. In this passage from Justice *he sees it as the worthless product of advanced capitalism.*

It is with a certain exultation that one walks through the wild jumble of inanity that clothes the walls of the Royal Academy to-day, when one thinks that the dominant class, the commercialist, noble and non-noble, who have deprived the people of art in their daily lives, can get for themselves nothing better than this for the satisfaction of their intellectual craving for beauty. . . . It is common for artists to prostitute their talents such as they are, not to popularity, which would be respectable comparatively, but to fortune-hunting: the ignorant public I have been mentioning is not the simple, uneducated public, but the cultured and guinea-shedding public.

Benson had been encouraged to take up metalwork by Morris and became managing director of the Company when Morris died. As a gentleman-craftsman, Benson was in many respects a figure typical of this new generation: a man who felt the need for his work to be displayed in a gallery rather than just a shop. Trade was still a social difficulty for many such people (though Benson had opened a shop by 1887) and the Arts and Crafts Exhibition Society was ideally suited to promoting such craftsmen, people whose aim was, in Benson's words: '. . . to produce work consistent and original in style, of shapely form, and carefully designed for the convenience of use.'

The first exhibition, held in 1888, was a successful and important event. Morris and Co displayed three tapestries from the *Morte d'Arthur* series, as well as chintzes, silks and carpets. De Morgan and Walter Crane also exhibited, while Mackmurdo and the Century Guild displayed thirty-four items. Among the other outstanding contributors were C. F. A Voysey and the furniture maker Ernest Gimson.

We have seen that Morris himself was involved in two influential types of furniture making: the lavishly decorated 'state' pieces such as the *St George's Cabinet* and what he called '... the necessary workaday furniture... which should... be well made and well proportioned, but simple to the last degree.' Of this latter type, the rush seated Sussex chairs, allegedly introduced by Warrington Taylor, were widely influential. Warrington Taylor himself clearly saw these as part of a social ideal. 'It is hellish wickedness,' he wrote to Webb, 'to spend more than 15/- on a chair when the poor are starving in the streets.' Webb's own furniture, much of which is highly distinguished, was open and honest in its construction and had a clear influence on such magnificent pieces as W. R Lethaby's sideboard, now in the Victoria and Albert Museum. This combines grace with functionalism, clear construction and restrained yet effective decoration. Ornament arising naturally out of construction is also clear in such pieces as Mackmurdo's elegant little writing desk with its chamfered legs and flat, square caps. Other Arts and Crafts furniture sometimes uses copper repoussé panels or the slightly more elegant and medieval inspired strapwork to be seen on Voysey's *Kelmscott Cabinet*, as well as fretted patterns of hearts, leaves and the ubiquitous tulip head.

Gimson's furniture was also concerned to reveal 'honest workmanship', whether in his vernacular inspired rush seated chairs or his more elaborate pieces. These are in some respects the equivalent of Morris's 'state furniture'. The best native woods are used in these pieces with the most refined appreciation of their natural qualities of colour and rhythm of grain. Ivory and mother of pearl escutcheons along with metal locks and handles provide the most enriching contrasts. It is in the detailing and design however that Gimson reveals the original yet timeless sense of proportion that places his best work on a level with the greatest English cabinet makers, thereby ensuring his place as one of the leading figures of the Arts and Crafts Movement.

A seminal range of talks was given in conjunction with the first Arts and Crafts exhibition, along with the publication of such essays as Walter Crane's 'Of the Revival of Design and Handicraft', in which he clearly expounded the philosophy of the movement. The division between artists and craftsmen is here decried, the new awareness of design made clear, while commercialism is once more attacked and handicraft praised. Morris himself wrote on tapestry and carpet weaving for the exhibition, while exhibiting some of his own calligraphy.

Cobden-Sanderson gave a talk on bookbinding, based on his experience at the Doves Bindery near Kelmscott House where he had bound Morris's own edition of *Capital*.

Above: *A writing table by A. H. Mackmurdo.*

Below: *A cabinet by Ernest Gimson.*

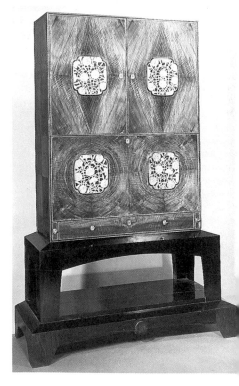

The profound influence of Morris's thought on the designers of his day can be seen in this section from 'Of the Revival of Design and Handicraft' by Walter Crane. It was published in the catalogue of the 1888 Arts and Crafts Exhibition.

The decorative artist and the handicraftsman have hitherto had but little opportunity of displaying their work in the public eye, or rather of appealing to it upon strictly artistic grounds in the same sense as the pictorial artist; and it is a somewhat singular state of things that at a time when the Arts are perhaps more looked after, and certainly more talked about, than they had ever been before, and the beautifying of houses, to those to whom it is possible, has become in some cases almost a religion, so little is known of the actual designer and maker. . . . It is undeniable that under the modern industrial system that personal element, which is so important in all forms of Art, has been thrust further and further into the background, until the production of what are called ornamental objects, and the supply of ornamental additions generally, instead of growing out of organic necessities, have become, under a misapplication of machinery, driven by the keen competition of trade, purely commercial affairs. . . . The true root and basis of all Arts lies in the handicrafts. If there is no room or chance of recognition for really artistic power and feeling in design and craftsmanship—if Art is not recognized in the humblest object and material, and felt to be as valuable in its own way as the more highly rewarded pictorial skill—the arts cannot be in a sound condition; and if artists cease to be found among the crafts there is great danger that they will vanish from the arts also, and become manufacturers and salesmen instead.

Cobden-Sanderson's aim in his work was in the true Arts and Crafts spirit of raising a technique to its highest status: a technique whereby a man regardless of his class might effect '. . . the union of the highest flight of the imagination and of the spirit, with the labour of the hands'. Oscar Wilde, who reported the talk for the *Pall Mall Gazette*, found Cobden-Sanderson's practical demonstration of bookbinding more impressive than his rhetoric, but the most influential lecture of the whole series was undoubtedly that by Emery Walker on letterpress printing which, as we have seen, was to inspire Morris to set up the Kelmscott Press.

While the beauty of the Kelmscott books is beyond question, Morris's attempt to create a 'pocket cathedral' in which the eye and mind can wander in search of ever new delights was less influential than the fact that a craftsman of his calibre had dedicated himself so fully to the technique. Indeed, even Mackail objected to the comparative difficulty of reading some of Morris's typefaces, while Morris's essentially backward looking printing processes could not be readily adapted to the great advances then being made in the production of books.

The Arts and Crafts movement was to be deeply impressed by his achievement nonetheless, particularly with his concern over the quality of materials. *The Hobby Horse* was also influential on graphic design, while *The Dial* became a vehicle for the innovative designs of Charles Ricketts. Ricketts also published in *The Yellow Book*, that quintessential work of the 1890s, which included illustrations by Image, Crane, Horne and Aubrey Beardsley whose black and white drawings for an edition of Malory, Morris frankly despised.

Commercial publishing houses, such as John Lane, were also interested in the new upsurge in typography, as were Dent, Methuen and William Heinemann. Morris's example was most crucial however on the Private Press Movement. Here, Hornby's Ashdene Press and the Vale Press produced such excellent work as the reprint of Drayton's *Nimphidia and the Muses*, with its beautifully flowing development of the Morris border. Books of high quality were also produced by the Eragny and Essex House Presses. Work of the greatest purity and influence was again produced by those who had worked most closely with Morris. In particular, Cobden-Sanderson and Emery Walker at the Doves Press issued their mighty Bible in 1905: clear, austere, and occasionally employing dramatic contrasts of colour.

Further exhibitions were held, and while the work of the Glasgow four—Charles Rennie Mackintosh, Herbert Macknair and Margaret and Frances Macdonald—showed how far into the difficult future some designers had already gone, the profound influence that Morris exerted on the younger generation became ever clearer. Nowhere is this more poignantly expressed than in the tribute paid to Morris by the *Studio* in its review of the exhibition of 1896, given after Morris's death: 'Looking at the beautiful objects which his enterprise had made possible,' the reviewer wrote, 'one felt that although the master had been taken, the principles he had established were so firmly rooted, that the legend of William Morris would be the creed of the new movement, and loyal adherence to his teaching would rank more than ever as its watchword.' English design had found its great master and, standing on his shoulders, English designers, as W. A. S. Benson realised:

> . . . are recognised in Europe as the exponents of the only vital modern style, a style still immature, and the nature of things not reaching immediate perfection all round; but in the main logical, consistent, and progressive. Though we cannot calculate on the uprise of any commanding genius to vie with the memory of those whose loss we are lamenting, that the number of capable artists is steadily increasing is evident from the list of contributors to this autumn's exhibition at the New Gallery.

One of the earliest foreign observers of this development was Herman Muthesius who was attached to the German Embassy to report on English housing. Fired by the 'pure and perfect utility' of the English style and impressed particularly by what he saw as the elegance of work now being made by designers for the machine, Muthesius realised how it was the ideals of William Morris that had prepared the ground for the creations of Germany's greatest commercial rival. These were opinions Muthesius expressed both in his book *Das Englische Haus* and in his lectures.

By 1907, these had inspired German trade associations to set up the Deutsche Werkbund with the aim of 'selecting the best representatives of art, industry, crafts and trades, of combining all efforts towards high quality in industrial work, and of forming a rallying-point for all those who are able and willing to work for high quality.' Similar bodies, equally concerned with the quality of machine production advocated by many of Morris's followers, soon sprang up on the continent, in Germany, Switzerland and Sweden.

In Germany, the movement spread rapidly under the influence of Muthesius and such men as Peter Behrens, Bruno Paul and van de Velde. By the outbreak of the First World War, Morris's emphasis on craft and his followers' attempts to unite this with the creative use of the machine had been synthesised in the work of Walter Gropius. By 1919, such ideas had been embodied in the teaching of the Staatliches Bauhaus, the true centre of modernism in design.

Another important figure to be deeply influenced by Morris and his followers was the American Gustav Stickley who, after a visit to England in 1899, set up his United Crafts workshops near Syracuse, New York.

These were later renamed the Craftsman Workshops and Stickley defined their aim as being:

> . . . to extend the principles established by Morris, in both the artistic and the socialistic sense. In the interests of art, they seek to substitute the luxury of taste for the luxury of costliness; to teach that beauty does not imply elaboration or ornament; to employ only those forms and materials which make for simplicity, individuality and dignity of effect.

Such ideas were further advanced through Stickley's journal *The Craftsman*, and so successful was his campaign that he too had to come to terms with the machine, using it as Morris might have wished: to do away with repetitious labour and so free the craftsman to concentrate on more important matters. This was to be a characteristic of the greater part of the American Arts and Crafts or 'craftsman' movement.

Stickley's furniture reveals its construction and emphasises its materials in a way familiar from the English Arts and Crafts Movement. Function and decoration are integrated while, just as English furniture makers had drawn on vernacular models, so Stickley himself was influenced by such traditional American styles as the profoundly beautiful furniture produced by the religious community of Shakers. Again, Stickley was concerned to emphasise the 'democratic' nature of his furniture: its simple, direct and non-elitist approach to design and manufacture. To this end, he opened up his twelve-storey Craftsman Building in New York City, an enterprise which was eventually to bankrupt him.

Below: *The revealed construction of this table by G. Stickley shows the influence of the Arts and Crafts Movement in America.*

Other American designers such as Elbert Hubbard and Charles Rohlfs were also to produce craftsman furniture, but many of the more distinguished pieces were the work of architects. This is particularly true of the furniture designed by the

Greene brothers in their work for the Gamble House, Pasadena, California. Charles Sumner Greene had visited England in 1901 to see the latest in design, but the work that he and his brother produced was far from dependent on this source alone. The Greene brothers realised how cabinet makers of the Far East had developed the most sophisticated approaches to design and the use of material. The Gamble House itself uses much of what they learned to great effect. Indeed, the result is a building of the most outstanding quality, deeply imaginative in conception, exquisite in its attention to detail, chaste yet sumptuous in its effects. C. R. Ashbee rightly described the furniture of the Greenes as 'tender, subtle, self-effacing and refined,' and it is an indication of the profound originality that American craftsmen could bring to these traditions.

Oriental influences can again be seen in the work of the American Prairie School who, like the Greenes and the designers of the English Arts and Crafts Movement, were also concerned to create harmonious and integrated interiors. While Louis Sullivan, the founder of the Prairie School, is perhaps best known for his commercial buildings, his followers such as George Grant Emslie and George Washington Maher produced domestic schemes of great interest, Maher's concern with integrated design extending as far as making furniture whose motifs are echoed in the architecture of the houses in which it is placed.

In the work of Frank Lloyd Wright, the greatest figure of the Prairie School, this theme of integrated design is seminal. 'The "grammar" of the house,' he wrote, 'is the manifest articulation of all its parts—the "speech" it uses . . . . Everything has a related articulation in relation to the whole and all belongs together because all are speaking the same language.' Wright himself was a founding member of the Chicago Arts and Crafts Society and he was deeply influenced by the organic ideals of the movement. The geometric also played an important part in his design work as did his response to landscape. In his designs for furniture, Wright also openly embraced the machine and was less interested in a handcrafted look. The energy of Wright's genius was such however that he could absorb ideas from the widest range of sources and produce work which, while it owes much to its craftsman origins, is yet a unique and timeless contribution to the history of Western cabinetmaking.

Just as the English Arts and Crafts Movement gave rise to a number of guilds and communities, so the American craftsman ideal inspired such associations as the Byrdcliffe Colony and Chicago's Hull House which aimed to teach craft skills to immigrants. One of the most successful of these associations was the New York Society of Decorative Art, founded as an 'American Kensington School' by the redoubtable Candace Wheeler. This was principally concerned with needlework, and its products include Wheeler's own magnificent *Consider the Lilies of the Field*, a *portière* embroidered on muslin for the highly influential home of Mark Twain. While original in their design, the motto running along the top is clearly derived from Morris's tapestry work.

In 1879, Candace Wheeler went into partnership with Louis Comfort Tiffany to create Associated Artists, a major American interior decorating firm. While much of Tiffany's work was influenced by Art Nouveau, Wheeler herself was an important figure in the recovery of such vernacular traditions as quilting as well as technical advances in weaving. Others were to follow her lead, Ellen Miller and Margaret Whiting founding for example the Society of Blue and White Needlework. The great tradition of American embroidery was thereby revived and placed on a sure foundation.

In addition to making furniture, Elbert Hubbard, founder of the Roycroft Shops, had visited Morris at the Kelmscott Press in 1894, and this interest helped make him one of the great influences on American craftsman printing. The *Inland Printer* had also publicised Morris's work in this field, while further magazines such as the *Knight Errant* and the *Studio* showed their interest in the Kelmscott Press and the achievements of *The Hobby Horse*. In 1891, Roberts Brothers of Boston issued an influential facsimile of *The Story of the Glittering Plain*. As in England, however, designers inspired by the work of the Kelmscott Press gradually simplified their work. Private presses also flourished, thereby establishing Morris's influence on American typographical design, an influence which persists to this day.

Indeed, Morris's presence is still felt in innumerable ways. Of all English designers, his is the work that remains perhaps the most readily recognised. Diaries, address books and students' folders are bound with copies of his papers. Morris textiles cover countless chairs and hang at innumerable windows. His work is consistently popular. It is of high quality and it is practical. Time too has given it something of the imagined appeal of a vanished age.

But there is surely a deeper allure to Morris's work than a sentimental fashion for the supposed security of Victorian values—values which Morris himself heartily despised. His best work breathes an awareness of nature and history that is both deeply felt and deeply thought. It is an act of faith on which the whole of his titanic energies were brought to bear, a profound statement about our place in nature and the dignity and freedom for which we crave. In the end, Morris himself saw no division between being a maker and a thinker, a designer of wallpaper and a political activist. All these pursuits were part of his concern to

Above: *Frank Lloyd Wright's office interior clearly shows the harmonious integration of all its elements.*

criticise his world in the hope of fashioning a better life for everyone. That search for joy and justice is still very potent, and today, when we hang Morris's fabrics in the ferro-concrete jungle, we pay a personal tribute to his search for value amid materialism.

Right: *A colophon designed by William Morris for books published by the Kelmscott Press.*

BIBLIOGRAPHY

WRITINGS BY WILLIAM MORRIS

The standard edition of William Morris's writings are the twenty-four volumes of *The Collected Works*, edited by May Morris and published in London between 1910–15. May Morris also produced two supplementary volumes: *William Morris: Artist, Writer, Socialist*, published by Blackwell, Oxford, 1936. *The Letters of William Morris to his Family and Friends* were edited by Philip Henderson, London, 1950. See also *The Collected Letters of William Morris*, vol. I, 1848–80, Princeton, 1984. *The Unpublished Lectures of William Morris* have been edited by Eugene D. Lemire, Michigan, 1969.

Useful selections of Morris's writings include: *William Morris, Stories in Prose, Stories in Verse, Shorter Poems, Lectures and Essays*, Century Edition, edited. G. D. H. Cole, New York, 1934; *William Morris: News from Nowhere and Selected Writings and Designs*, edited by Asa Briggs, with a Supplement by Graeme Shankland on William Morris, Designer, Harmondsworth, 1984; *A Choice of William Morris's Verse*, selected with an Introduction by Geoffrey Grigson, London, 1969; *Political Writings of William Morris*, edited with an Introduction by A. L. Morton, London, 1973; *William Morris by Himself, Designs and Drawings*, edited Gillian Naylor, London, 1988, also contains a selection of Morris's writings and is profusely illustrated.

BIOGRAPHIES OF WILLIAM MORRIS

The earliest biography of William Morris is J.W. Mackail: *The Life of William Morris*, London, 1899. Modern biographies include: E. P. Thompson, *William Morris: Romantic to Revolutionary*, London, 1955, rev. ed. 1977, the definitive study of his political life; Paul Thompson, *The Work of William Morris*, London, 1967, which is also an excellent introduction to the spectrum of Morris's work; Philip Henderson, *William Morris, his Life, Work and Friends*, London, 1967, rev. ed. 1977, which is the essential modern biography; Ian Bradley, *William Morris and his World*, London, 1978; Peter Faulkner, *Against the Age, An Introduction to William Morris*, London, 1980, which is particularly strong on Morris as a writer. Peter Faulkner has also edited *William Morris: The Critical Heritage*, London, 1973, a valuable record of contemporary opinions of Morris. A fine brief biography is *William Morris* by Paul Stansky, Oxford, 1983.

STUDIES OF MORRIS'S WORK

The most useful general introduction is Paul Thompson, *The Work of William Morris*, London, 1967. This may be supplemented by Ray Watkinson's more generously illustrated *William Morris as Designer*, New York, 1967, and *William Morris by Himself, Designs and Drawings*, edited Gillian Naylor, London, 1988.

For Morris's work in stained glass see A. C. Sewter, *The Stained Glass of William Morris and his Circle*, London and New York, 2 vols, 1974.

For Morris's printed and woven designs, see: Fiona Clark, *William Morris: Wallpaper and Chintzes*, London, 1973; Oliver Fairclough and Emeline Leary, *Textiles by William Morris and Morris and Co.*, London, 1981; Linda Parry, *William Morris Textiles*, London, 1983, and the same author's *William Morris and the Arts and Crafts Movement: A Design Source Book*, which includes an essay on the textiles of the American Arts and Crafts Movement by Gillian Moss, London, 1989.

For houses decorated by Morris, see: Mark Girouard, *The Victorian Country House*, New Haven and London, 1979.

For Morris's printed books, see: H. H. Sparling, *The Kelmscott Press and William Morris, Master-craftsman*, London, 1924; Rauri McLean, *Victorian Book Design*, London, 1963, and *Modern Book Design*, London, 1958; *The Typographical Adventure of William Morris*, William Morris Society, 1958.

Studies of Morris's literary work include: Peter Faulkner, *Against the Age, An Introduction to William Morris*, London, 1980; Delbert R. Gardner, *An 'Idle Singer' and his Audience*, The Hague and Paris, 1975; Roderick Marshall, *William Morris and his Earthly Paradise*, Tisbury, 1979; Amanda Hodgson, *The Romances of William Morris*, Cambridge, 1987.

Morris's influence on the Arts and Crafts Movement is assessed in Peter Stansky, *Redesigning the World, William Morris, the 1880s, and the Arts and Crafts*, Princeton, 1985.

BACKGROUND STUDIES

Useful studies of England in 1851 and of the Great Exhibition are: Asa Briggs, *Victorian People: A Reassessment of Persons and Themes, 1851–67*, 1954, Harmondsworth, 1965, as well as his *Victorian Things*, London, 1988; J. Steegman, *Victorian Taste, A Study of the Arts and Architecture from 1830 to 1870*, London, 1970; Nikolaus Pevsner, *High Victorian Design, A Study of the Exhibits of 1851*, London, 1951; Eric de Mare, *London 1851, the Year of the Great Exhibition*, London, 1973; C. H. Gibbs-Smith, *The Great Exhibition of 1851*, London, 1950. A useful modern approach to art and industrialism is Adrian Forty, *Objects of Desire, Design and Society*, London, 1986. Bernard Denvir, *The Late Victorians: Art, Design and Society*, Harlow, 1986, offers a useful series of contemporary readings.

Useful studies of the Pre-Raphaelites include: William Gaunt, *The Pre-Raphaelite Tragedy*, London, 1942; Timothy Hilton, *The Pre-Raphaelites*, London, 1970; Jan Marsh, *Pre-Raphaelite Sisterhood*, London, 1985, and her *Pre-Raphaelite Women*, London, 1987. A useful and well-illustrated monograph is *Burne-Jones* by Martin Harrison and Bill Waters, London, rev. ed. 1977.

Studies of other contemporary figures to influence Morris are: George P. Landow, *Ruskin*, Oxford, 1985. 'The Nature of Gothic' is most readily accessible in '*Unto This Last' and Other Writings*, edited with an introduction and commentary by Clive Wilmer, Harmondsworth, 1985. A. L. Le Quesne, *Carlyle*, Oxford, 1982 and *Thomas Carlyle: Selected Writings*, edited with an Introduction by Alan Shelston, Harmondsworth, 1971. Peter Singer, *Marx*, Oxford, 1980. There is an edition of Samuel Moore's translation of *The Communist Manifesto*, edited by A. J. P. Taylor, Harmondsworth, 1967, while see also *Karl Marx: Selected Writings in Sociology and Social Philosophy*, edited and translated by T. B. Bottomore and Maximilien Rubel, pbk ed. Harmondsworth, 1963.

For the influence of the Victoria and Albert Museum on Morris, see Barbara Morris, *Inspiration for Design: the Influence of the Victoria and Albert Museum*, London, 1986.

For the Arts and Crafts Movement, see: Gillian Naylor, *The Arts and Crafts Movement*, London, 1971; Peter Stansky, *Redesigning the World, William Morris, the 1880s, and the Arts and Crafts*, Princeton, 1985; Linda Parry, *Textiles of the Arts and Crafts Movement*, London, 1988, and the same author's *William Morris and the Arts and Crafts Movement: A Design Source Book*, London, 1989; *Encyclopedia of Arts and Crafts: The International Arts Movement 1850–1920*, consultant, Wendy Caplan, London, 1989. For the international perspective, see: Nikolaus

Pevsner, *Pioneers of Modern Design from William Morris to Walter Gropius* pbk ed. Harmondsworth, 1975 and *Treasures of the American Arts and Crafts Movement, 1890–1920*, Tod M. Volpe, Beth Cathers with text by Alastair Duncan and Introduction by Leslie Bowman, London, 1988.

PICTURE CREDITS

INDEX

Page numbers in italics refer to captions to illustrations